RYA
for ~~Sail a~~

By Rob Gibson

Illustrations by Andrew Simpson

© Rob Gibson 2008
First Published 2008
The Royal Yachting Association
RYA House, Ensign Way, Hamble
Southampton SO31 4YA
Tel: 0845 345 0400
Fax: 0845 345 0329
E-mail: publications@rya .org.uk
Web: www.rya.org.uk
ISBN: 978-1-905-104-83-3
RYA Order Code: G68

Totally Chlorine   Sustainable
Free   Forests

A CIP record of this book is available from the British Library.

Note: While all reasonable care had been taken in the preparation
of this book, the publisher takes no responsibility for the use of the
methods or products or contracts described in the book.

Edited by: Andrew Simpson
Cover Design: Pete Galvin
Typesetting and Design: Kevin Slater
Proofreading and indexing: Alan Thatcher
Printed in China through World Print
Photographs: Andrew Simpson

FOREWORD

Completing the perfect manoeuvre is arguably one of the most satisfying aspects of going afloat. Indeed, I defy any helmsman not to admit, as their boat slides neatly into its berth or as their crew gently lift the mooring buoy, that they do not feel just a little bit smug.

For good reason since they've just balanced a myriad number of forces by carefully exercising just a couple of controls with perhaps a little extra jiggery-pokery with a warp and a fender.

When it comes to boat handling, no two situations are ever the same. Even if you only ever take your boat to and from your regular mooring. The wind may be stronger or weaker or coming from a slightly different direction, the tide may be flowing or ebbing at a different rate, the loading of the boat and even the movement of the crew will affect the way the boat moves through the water. With so many different forces acting in various ways, it is a wonder we are ever able to leave let alone make a safe return.

The secret is taking the time to assess the situation and make a plan of action in accordance with the 'rules'.

That's why this book is so valuable. It explains the process not only for day-to-day manoeuvring but also in emergencies - when failure is not an option.

With its clear illustrations and pragmatic approach, it describes the practical aspects of boat handling, providing guidelines that will stand you in good stead for every circumstance.

Practice the advice given here and before long you too will be standing at the helm with a self-satisfied smile. I guarantee it.

Keith Colwell
RNLI Divisional Sea Safety Manager – South
Author of RYA Sea Survival Handbook

INTRODUCTION

In open water, away from land and an audience, you can make as many mistakes as you like and simply shrug them off. As most of us have discovered, the really embarrassing moments come when things go wrong in the marina or harbour – usually under the critical scrutiny of your fellow sailors who, while being sympathetic with your misfortunes, are unlikely to let you forget them. Most sailors agree that it is the 'take offs and landings' that are the most difficult and stressful operations. So the object of this book is to take the stress out of those situations by gaining a fuller understanding of how to deal with the challenges in a thoughtful and logical way.

A wide variety of common situations are described and analysed, but it is impracticable to include every obscure possibility that might confront us. However, once the general principles are understood, you will find yourself better equipped to face any boat handling challenge by applying the basic rules for whichever type of boat – sail or power – under your command. I hope after reading this book you will agree that good boat handling is all about awareness of the forces at work, plus the application of a few simple techniques.

Throughout, the word 'sailors' refers to powerboaters as well, and 'he' or 'helmsman' has been adopted for simplicity's sake and could just as easily be 'she' or 'helmswoman'.

Happy landings!

Key to symbols used in illustrations throughout the book

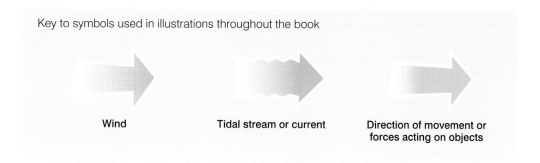

Wind   Tidal stream or current   Direction of movement or
                                             forces acting on objects

---

CONTENTS

1 PRINCIPLES AND PROBLEMS   6

Boat types   7
Tides and currents   8
Use the stream to advantage   9
Wind   10
Prop walk   11
Momentum   12
Principles of control   13
   Twin screws   14
   Steerable drives   14
   Going astern   14

2 BASIC MANOEUVRES   15

Sitting in a tideway   15
Making turns   16
Slow speed control   18
Fast turns   19
Picking up buoys   20
Securing to buoys   21
Making fast   22
Coming alongside a tidal
quay wall   23
The ferry glide   24
Lines of approach   25
Leaving a wall or pontoon   27
   Springing off   28

3 INTO THE MARINA   29

Planning   29
   Mid-ships spring   30
Head to stream   31
Head to stream, turn first   32
Downstream   33

Downstream, stop and reverse   34
Still water, leeward finger berth   35
Windward finger berth   36
Windward finger berth with
stream under pontoon   37
General advice   38

4 OUT OF THE MARINA   39

Getting ready to go   39
   Singling up   39
      Upstream exit   40
      Downstream exit   41
Using warps to advantage   42
Taming the prop walk effect   44
Wind off the pontoon   45
Gale from ahead   46

**5 BOAT TYPES AND
    THEIR LIMITATIONS   47**

Sailing cruiser   47
Racing yachts   47
Long keeled sailing yachts   48
Single screw motor boats   48
Twin engine boats   49
Steerable drive boats   49
Outboard variations   49

**6 ROPES, KNOTS,
    CLEATS AND BOLLARDS   50**

Ropes   50
Cleats and bollards   51
Knots   52

7 MOORINGS	54
Alongside a tidal quay	54
Non-tidal moorings and floating pontoons	55
Trot moorings	56
Approach for twin engine and steerable drive boats	57
Approach for single screw boats	58
Stern-to moorings	58
Lazy lines	60
Rafting	61
Leaving a raft	62

8 HANDLING UNDER SAIL	63
Selecting the best line of approach	64
Downwind and upstream	64
Upwind and upstream	65
Scandalising	66
Sailing onto quays or pontoons	67
Onshore wind ahead	67
Wind abaft the beam	68
Offshore wind just forward of the beam	68
Surging	69
Sailing off	69
Heaving to	70
Downwind sailing	71
Preventers	71
Rolling	71
Poling out headsails	72
Mainsail or no mainsail	72
Twin headsails	72
Motor sailing	73

9 ANCHORING	74
Choosing an anchorage	74
Rope or chain	76
Coming to anchor	77
Sailing to anchor	78
Raising the anchor	78

10 TOWING	80
Alongside tows	81

11 HEAVY WEATHER	82
Weather forecasts	83
Breaking waves and broaching	84
Drogues	85
Storm and heavy weather sails	86
Driving over waves	88
Motor yacht	88
Sailing yacht	89

12 EMERGENCIES	90
Groundings	90
Man overboard (MOB)	92
Sailing cruisers	94
Sailing yachts with large mainsails	95
Large motor boats	96
RIBs and small powerboats	97
Lifebuoys, danbuoys and lights	98
Helicopter rescue	99

GLOSSARY	100

INDEX	104

1 PRINCIPLES AND PROBLEMS

Everybody who has handled a boat of any type in close quarters will agree that all sorts of outside forces contrive to wrest control of the vessel from your hands. So a good starting point is to know just what those outside forces are. Once you understand the effect they have, you can anticipate – or at least react in a proper manner – to their combined influences. What's more, you can even take advantage of them – employing them as additional controls to help put the boat where you want it.

The forces are: TIDE, WIND, PROP WALK and MOMENTUM.

Clearly, the combination of these effects will change with the conditions of the day. Also every boat has its individual handling characteristics that must be understood and allowed for. However, once you understand how your boat will behave in every situation, and get into the habit of applying whichever 'golden rules' are best for each particular circumstance, you will find that your confidence and success rate will soar.

Before we move on to the influence of tide, wind, prop walk and momentum, let's deal briefly with the various types of boats and how in general you can expect them to handle. Techniques for taking advantage of their strengths and overcoming their weaknesses will be covered in much greater detail later. Because some of the phraseology may not be familiar, you might find it helpful to refer to the glossary or section dealing with those specific points for further information.

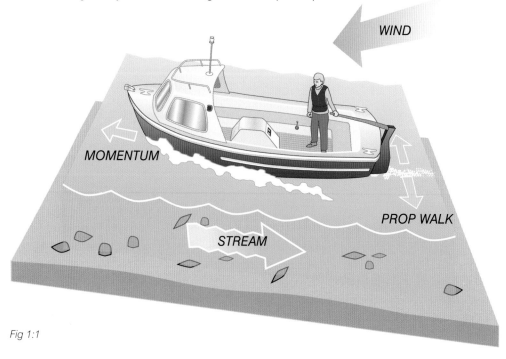

Fig 1:1

BOAT TYPES – HOW WILL THEY HANDLE?

Fin or twin keeled sailing yachts

With the propeller well aft and close to the rudder, steering under power is excellent when motoring forward. However, reversing is nothing like as positive, but improves with a little more speed. Having the propeller so far aft means that the effects of prop walk are significant (see page 11).

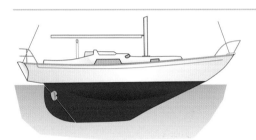

Long keeled sailing yachts

The long keel underwater profile is great for sailing in straight lines but manoeuvrability in marinas was never part of the design brief. Not surprisingly, this traditional type is awkward in close quarters – particularly when going astern.

Single screw motorboats

These have powerful fixed propellers but relatively small rudders. They handle well when going forward but are much less manoeuvrable going astern – even less than a fin or twin keeled sailing yacht. The size and position of the prop makes prop walk an important control.

Twin screw motorboats

This category includes larger power craft and catamarans with an engine in each hull.

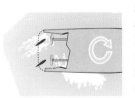 Since the engines can be operated independently – one powering ahead, the other astern, for example – these boats are highly manoeuvrable in all respects.

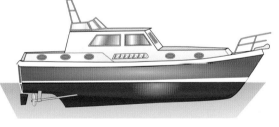

Steerable drive motorboats

These do not have rudders but steer by directing the prop thrust to push or pull their sterns from side to side. With the engine (or engines) put in neutral a steerable drive boat will simply continue to drift in the direction that it was last driven until the momentum dies away. Single engined boats of this type are much less manoeuvrable than twin engined designs.

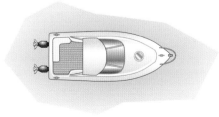

TIDES AND CURRENTS

Whenever we get involved in close quarters manoeuvring, there is nearly always some form of tidal flow or river current. Awareness of the tidal situation should be a fundamental part of passage planning for the offshore sailor but, in inshore waters, relying on flow charts and other predictions can be misleading since eddying streams will often do the unexpected. Incidentally, from here on we shall use the word 'stream' to mean both tides and currents unless there's a good reason to be more specific.

Either way, it is what's happening around you at any moment in time that's important, so get into the habit of being observant – look for evidence of the local situation continuously. Here are some clues:

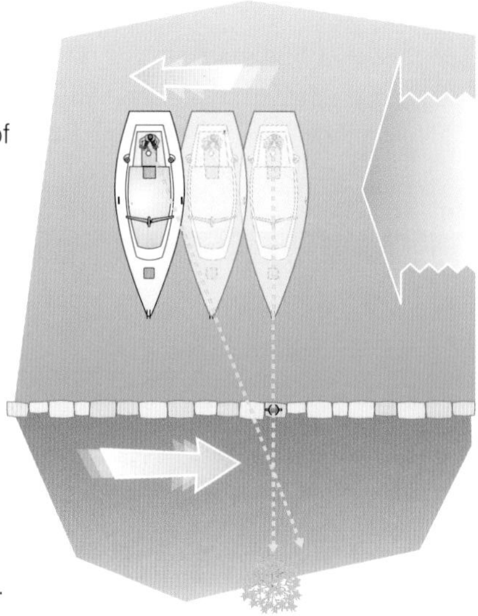

- Unless influenced by a very strong wind, the stream will cause moored boats to tug at either their stern or bow lines.

- You may see the stream surging around pilings or dangling ropes.

Fig 1:2

- If at anchor or alongside, there could be flotsam moving downtide or underwater weed flowing from the underside of the pontoon.

- If underway you can stall the boat at ninety degrees to the expected flow and note which way she drifts compared with any nearby land. (See Fig 1:2)

- When you turn into the tide, the boat will seem to pivot around the bow and you will gain control as you turn, whereas, when you turn downtide, the boat will seem to pivot around the stern, and you will feel the current carrying you away.

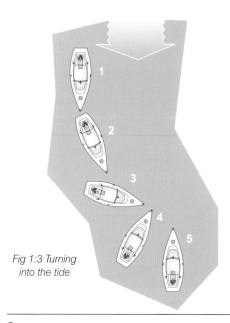

Fig 1:3 Turning into the tide

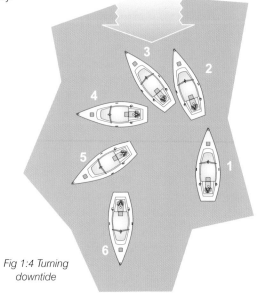

Fig 1:4 Turning downtide

USE THE STREAM TO ADVANTAGE

Imagine you are adrift in a river with a current flowing at 2 knots. You will have no steerage or any other control over the boat, but you will still be in danger of hitting rocks, buoys, anchored boats or anything else fixed to the ground – and you will hit them at 2 knots, the speed of the stream. This is not a great situation. But if instead you turn to point the boat upstream and motor ahead at 2 knots, you will find yourself in the happy position of having zero impact speed with those same objects and, with 2 knots of flow passing over your rudder, you will remain in perfect control.

So, the first and most important golden rule is to **STEER INTO THE CURRENT.**

At this point, you may be thinking that you know an instance where that rule wouldn't apply – but the fact is it can – in all circumstances, at least in terms of making the final contact. You will often hear it said that when making your approach you should head into a strong wind and ignore a weak current. But this is bad advice because it ignores the fact that your main control is your rudder, which is totally unaffected by the wind and only works when there's water flowing past it (see page 13). Of course, you can't ignore the wind, as we shall see in the next section, but it's the stream that provides the ultimate control.

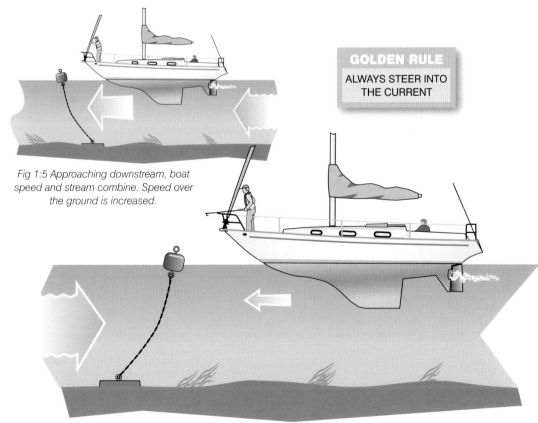

GOLDEN RULE
ALWAYS STEER INTO THE CURRENT

Fig 1:5 Approaching downstream, boat speed and stream combine. Speed over the ground is increased.

Fig 1:6 Approaching upstream, boat speed over the ground is reduced

WIND

Boats have tremendous windage. A brisk breeze can play on the hull sides, superstructure and rigging with sufficient force to propel a mid-size sailing cruiser through the water at over a knot without a scrap of sail up. Knowing the wind direction should be part of your overall

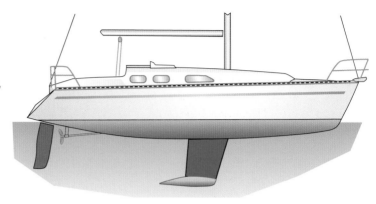

Fig 1:7

awareness and there are lots of indicators such as flags, smoke from chimneys, the advance of waves on the water and so on to tell us which way it's blowing. Even seagulls – all but the most stupid stand facing the wind – are there to give us guidance.

So we must expect our boats to be blown away by the wind – and in a predictable manner. Figure 1:7 shows a yacht in profile. Notice how the forward sections have relatively less area in the water than further aft – less 'grip' in effect. In this case we can expect the bow to blow away from the wind more readily than the rest of the boat. If, say, you were trying to keep station in a tideway, perhaps waiting for a bridge to open, you should expect even a light wind to blow your bow away and might find yourself having to nudge it back up by steering upwind with short bursts of power.

Motorboats, particularly those with planing hulls and high topsides, typically have more windage and even less grip and are notoriously prone to being blown sideways (see Fig 1:8 below). A strong wind can make coming alongside a 'weather berth' very awkward, but don't despair. If you're aware of the wind direction and what it's likely to do to your boat then you can deal with it and even use it to your advantage.

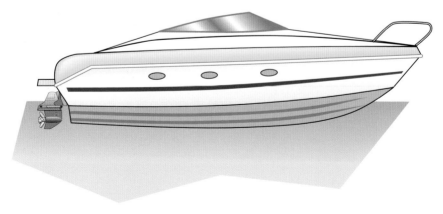

Fig 1:8

As a basic rule we should try to either steer directly into the wind or directly away from it (Fig 1:9). Most sailing cruisers will prefer the former. As long as the direction is well judged, the boat can easily be held head to wind even at low boat speeds. Single screw (or outdrive) motor boats will probably prefer to reverse into a strong wind allowing the wind to keep the bow of the boat pointing downwind like a weather vane while the boat 'hangs' on the prop. It makes no difference to twin screw motor boats and catamarans which way they choose to face the wind, but they should always use forward and reverse thrust rather than their rudders to steer at low speeds.

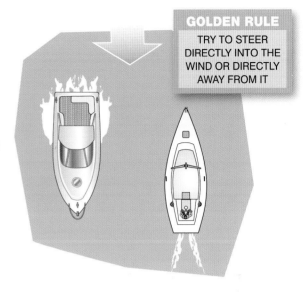

GOLDEN RULE
TRY TO STEER DIRECTLY INTO THE WIND OR DIRECTLY AWAY FROM IT

Fig 1:9

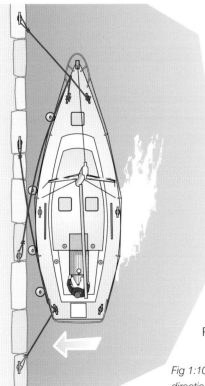

PROP WALK

This phenomenon, sometimes called the 'paddle wheel effect' or simply 'the kick', is caused by energy spiralling off the propeller blade tips as they spin. When motoring forwards, if the helm is left unattended most boats will slowly circle. This circling is a result of prop walk, but is so easily countered by steering that it can be ignored. In reverse, however, the situation is very different. When reverse power is applied, all the propeller's thrust is directed away from the rudder, effectively leaving you without steerage until you build up speed through the water. At the same time the prop walk is maximised and will throw the stern of the boat in one direction or the other before 'steerage way' is regained. But remember, the effect is caused by the spinning propeller, so to stop the effect simply PUT THE ENGINE IN NEUTRAL.

Fig 1:10 In reverse gear, prop walk works in the opposite direction to the emerging wash

As we mentioned earlier (page 7) some boats have less prop walk than others. For example, many racing yachts have propellers just behind their keels, almost at mid-length and close to the boat's pivot point. Although such propellers still produce prop walk, the effect on steering is minimal. In fact, prop walk is really a feature of fixed single screw boats where the propeller is set well aft, but, for those vessels, the effect is significant, particularly in reverse. In reality we only consider the effect of prop walk when we are going astern so from here on, when 'the kick' is referred to, it means the effects of prop walk in reverse gear.

When you take a boat out for the first time, it's almost inevitable that your first manoeuvre will be to reverse out of a finger berth. In which case it will be really handy to be able to predict the direction and strength of the prop walk. To ascertain this, put the boat in reverse gear while it is still firmly moored up. Then look at the propeller wash, which will almost certainly surge out more strongly from under one side of the hull than the other. This tells you that the stern will kick in the opposite direction – and the greater the angle opened between the direction of the wash and the centre line of the boat, the more pronounced the kick will be.

NOTE: The majority of single screw boats kick to port so this is assumed to be the case in all of the manoeuvres described in this book.

MOMENTUM

The average family cruiser can weigh several tonnes. Given that they have relatively little grip in the water it's not surprising that they will skid sideways some distance when a tight turn is made. The skid is caused by momentum. It isn't dramatic or dangerous, but it can mean that you might not end up where you thought you would – perhaps in your neighbour's berth rather than your own or endlessly circling a mooring buoy without ever closing the gap.

Problems caused by momentum are common to all boat types. So, to avoid embarrassment, manoeuvre slowly and don't attempt pickups on the inside of a turn.

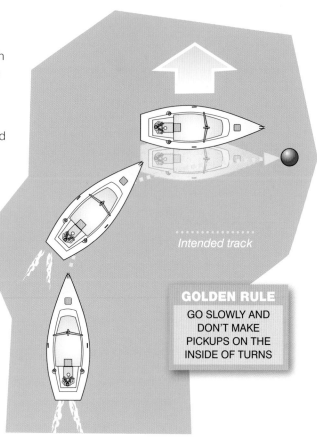

Intended track

GOLDEN RULE

GO SLOWLY AND DON'T MAKE PICKUPS ON THE INSIDE OF TURNS

Fig 1:11 Momentum will carry a boat outwards when you turn

PRINCIPLES OF CONTROL

Ask most beginners how a boat is controlled and they will point to the tiller or steering wheel. Well, that's almost right but the real control is the rudder, possibly unseen beneath the hull. Like all foils, in order for rudders to work they must have a flow of water passing over their blades. In the absence of any waterflow – say drifting, dead in the water – you have no control. But, the moment a waterflow is established you can steer, and the faster that waterflow becomes, the more powerful a rudder will be. So the skilled boat handler isn't constantly watching his or her hands on the wheel but has a clear mental picture of the rudder position and the flow of water passing over it. With the rudder set at an angle, the flow of water is deflected, 'lift' is created, and the stern of the boat will swing to one side.

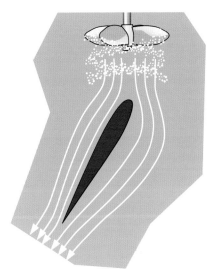

Fig 1:12 Rudders only work when there is waterflow over their blades

The second and – for most boaters – the only other control under engine is the propeller. Obviously the propeller is used to drive the boat forwards and backwards but, most importantly in boat handling, it's also used to make the rudder more effective by accelerating the waterflow over its blade.

By accelerating the flow briefly, you can take advantage of the rudder without moving the boat significantly forward. With the rudder to one side, a quick burst of the throttle in forward gear will push the stern sideways before the thrust overcomes the boat's inertia sufficiently for it to creep ahead. Figure 1:13 shows a typical modern sailing cruiser with a fin keel, a rudder set well back and the propeller close in front of it. In such circumstances, this type of boat will pivot around its keel easily. So, it's important to understand that you don't need waterflow over the whole hull to steer – just the rudder blade will do.

Single screw motorboats also have their propellers and rudders well aft so will behave similarly. However, they don't have fin keels so the natural pivot point is much further aft.

Pivot point

Fig 1:13 Sailing boats pivot somewhere around the leading edges of their keels. For motorboats, the pivot point is much further aft

GOLDEN RULE
STEER BEFORE GEAR. IN OTHER WORDS, POSITION YOUR RUDDER FIRST, THEN ACCELERATE.

Twin screws

Although twin screw motor vessels (including catamarans with an engine in each hull) will also have their rudders and props arranged close together, for tight manoeuvres they will normally leave their rudders amidships and use the forward/reverse facilities of both engines independently to pivot their boats – in these cases around a point just in front of the propellers.

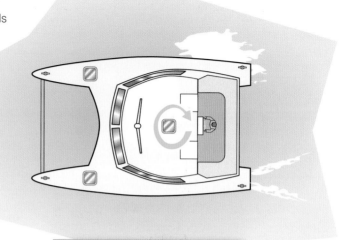

GOLDEN RULE

for twin screw craft:
WHEN MANOEUVRING IN CLOSE QUARTERS USE PROP THRUST RATHER THAN RUDDERS

Steerable drives

Vessels with outdrives or outboards only have one control mechanism – thrust, be it forward or reverse. The drive units are swivelled to direct the thrust and push or pull the stern around a pivot point just in front of the drive units. When manoeuvring at slow speed, these sailors, more than most, need to be mindful of the 'steer before gear' rule since, if they apply thrust before they have steered, the effect could be exactly the opposite of what they intended.

In close quarters, twin steerable drive vessels should act as if they had fixed drives – that's to say, put the helm amidships and then use forward and reverse to turn the boat.

Going astern

In forward gear the propeller is working at maximum efficiency, accelerating the waterflow over the rudder, so you have lots of control, even at very low boat speeds. When reversing, the propeller isn't so efficient, prop walk is maximised and rudder control depends on the flow of water generated by boat speed so control is not as good. If you need to reverse into a tight space, it helps to take a long run up to allow plenty of room, firstly to achieve steerage way and secondly to get a really good feel for how the boat is handling on the day. Single screw boats should be handled positively – that's to say, not too timidly – to maintain that all important flow over the rudder and give the best possible control. Excessive prop kick can be avoided by going into neutral and coasting occasionally and – if it all starts to happen too fast – a burst of forward thrust will stop you very effectively.

Twin screw boats should reverse using combinations of forward and reverse on their two motors, having just as much control astern as they have going forwards.

2 BASIC MANOEUVRES

SITTING IN A TIDEWAY

It's surprising how often that you need to sit still, waiting for locks or bridges to open or for a harbour master to tell you where to berth. Often you will be amongst a crowd of other yachts, so circling madly is simply not an option. In these circumstances, keeping control of your boat while staying 'on station' requires different combinations of rudder position and propeller thrust depending upon the interaction of wind and tide. So, here are some common examples:

1 The sailing cruiser has only a rudder and single engine at its disposal, but she also has a keel giving it lots of grip in the water and the ability to pivot around the centre point. The helmsman will be using short bursts of forward power to counter the stream, coupled with some port rudder to push the bow into the wind and prevent it from blowing away to starboard.

2 The motor yacht helm can use occasional bursts of forward thrust to counter the tide and short bursts of the bow thruster – if he has one – to hold the bow up against the wind. Without a bow thruster the motor cruiser must use port rudder and occasional bursts of forward thrust, again to counter the stream and keep the bow up into the wind.

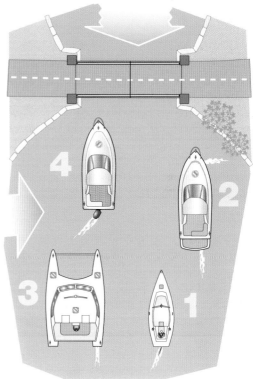

Fig 2:1

3 The catamaran with an engine in each hull can use short bursts of the starboard engine to both counter the tide and pivot the bows up into the wind.

4 The motor cruiser with a single outboard will use full port lock and occasional bursts of forward to nudge the bow up into the wind.

In a stronger wind and less tide, the helmsmen may choose to turn their boats towards the wind direction, allowing the tide on their starboard bow to keep their bows up into wind. But they would have to accept some tidal drift to port.

In this case (Fig 2:2), the tide is carrying the boats towards the closed bridge and the wind is on the starboard beam.

1 This time, the sailing cruiser (whose prop kicks to port) is using very gentle reverse thrust to hold the boat against the tide and minimise prop walk. The boat is being steered in reverse, so a little port rudder is needed to pivot the bow up into the wind.

2 Our motor yacht can use bursts of reverse thrust to hold it against the tide, coupled with bursts from the bow thruster to hold the bow against the wind.

3 The catamaran may use constant gentle reverse of the starboard engine to counter the tide with occasional bursts ahead or astern with the port engine to counter the wind effect.

4 The cruiser with the single outboard will need to use reverse with some port lock to pull the stern back into the tide and the bow up into the wind.

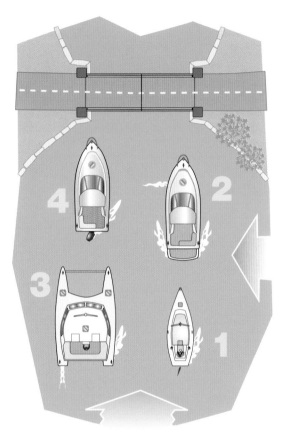

Fig 2:2

MAKING TURNS

For all helmsmen, the ability to turn a boat at almost zero speed and in little more than its own length is an absolutely vital skill. The manoeuvre should be practised before it's needed – ideally in open water where no damage will be caused should things go awry. Let's see how it might be required in real life.

Aboard our single screw yacht, we have entered a marina and drifted to a halt in the fairway, only to discover that the berth that we have been allocated is, in fact, filled (see Fig 2:3). There is no stream or significant wind to worry about.

Here's what to do (Fig 2:3):

1: **Give the boat full starboard helm and use a couple of short bursts of forward power to start her turning to starboard.**

2: **The moment you sense the boat moving forward, apply a good burst of astern power, still keeping the helm hard over to starboard. This will both kick your stern to port and pull the yacht backwards.**

3: **Repeat this sequence until you have turned 180° then motor serenely out the way you came.**

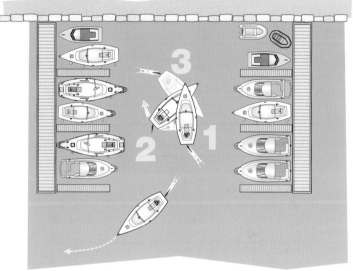

Fig 2:3

Twin screw motor yachts can achieve the same result by using forward gear on one engine and reverse on the other. It's worth repeating the fact that drivers of twin engine boats will, in close quarters manoeuvring, only use engine controls – leaving their rudders for steering at speed.

Now for a boat with a single steerable drive, drifted to a halt on the centreline of the fairway (Fig 2:4):

1: **Select full starboard lock and give a couple of bursts forward. The boat's stern will kick out to port turning the boat to starboard.**

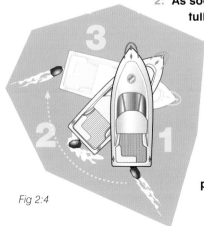

2: **As soon as you sense the boat moving forward, apply full port lock and give a couple of bursts astern. The stern will again kick to port and the boat will pull astern and the bow will effectively still be turning to starboard.**

3: **Full lock to starboard and a couple more forward bursts should complete the 180° turn. If not, repeat the sequence. Spinning the wheel from side to side is a more energetic process than on a fixed screw vessel, and one in which observance of the 'steer before gear' rule is paramount.**

Fig 2:4

SLOW SPEED CONTROL

In still water, as your boat slows down, there comes a point when the steering becomes ineffective and other effects – mainly the wind – will take control of the boat. It takes a lot of confidence to operate your boat below stall speed but there are situations when it has to be done.

Let's say you want to take your sailing cruiser alongside a quay wall, starboard side to. The wind is pushing the boat onto the wall. In Fig 2:5 an inexperienced helmsman has slowed the boat down nicely and then sensed the lack of rudder control as the wind started to push

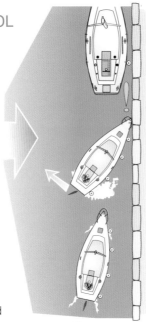

Fig 2:5

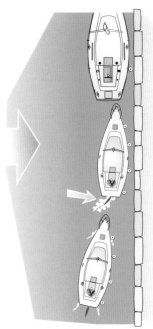

Fig 2:6

the bow towards the wall. Panicking, he engages reverse gear to take the last way off the boat. Unfortunately the stern then kicks to port and the bow, already being blown down by the wind, crashes into the wall.

In Fig 2:6, a more experienced helmsman makes much the same approach. However, when the boat slows and the steering stalls, instead of engaging reverse he applies full port rudder and gives a burst of power ahead. This throws the stern towards the wall and the bow out. The manoeuvre is completed by giving a short burst astern to take the last of the way off the boat.

Given the choice, it's much better for a single screw boat to moor on the same side as the direction of its propeller kick (Fig 2:7). You can then make your approach at a good angle to the quay or pontoon knowing that a good dose of reverse will both stop the boat and swing the stern towards the quay, bringing the bow out. This should square you up nicely and residual momentum will hold you against the wall for those few vital seconds while you secure the boat.

Although here we have concentrated on the single screw sailing cruiser, the moral applies to all boat types. When operating at below stall speed, set the steering, and know which way to apply thrust to regain control.

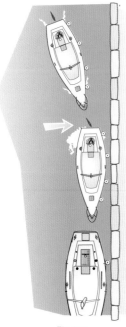

Fig 2:7

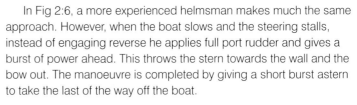

FAST TURNS

In emergencies, the propeller kick on a
single screw sailing boat can be used to
make fast, tight turns – but the effects can
be violent so try to make sure the cabin
table hasn't just been laid for tea.

■ Let's say you are motoring along at
somewhere between 2 to 5 knots.
Warn the crew!

■ Put the helm hard to starboard
and the engine into neutral. The
boat will start to turn.

■ Wait a couple of seconds or so
then go hard astern.

■ The effect will be dramatic: your
stern will be dragged to port by the
combination of reverse and prop
walk, while the resistance caused
by twisting the keel in the water
will take the way off the boat very
quickly.

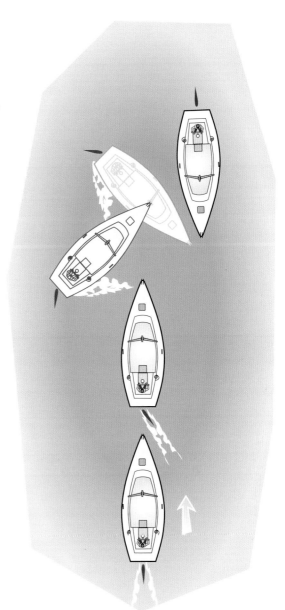

*Fig 2:8 Put the best china
away before you attempt this
manoeuvre!*

TIP Whenever you move your engine control from forward to reverse or vice versa,
pause in neutral for a couple of seconds. This allows your propeller shaft to stop spinning
one way before you ask it to spin in the other direction. Be kind to your gearbox and save
some expensive repair costs.

PICKING UP BUOYS – WIND AGAINST STREAM

A strong wind blowing in the opposite direction to the stream could be one situation where you might be tempted to ignore our first golden rule (page 9). DON'T. Always steer into the stream.

In this example (Fig 2:9) we're motoring towards a mooring buoy facing a 2 knot tide, with a near gale blowing from astern. The wind is pushing us forward at an alarming rate. At 20 metres (66 feet) from the buoy we engage reverse gear to slow the boat down. At 5 metres (16.4 feet) we increase the reverse thrust so that the boat is slowed further until the bow is held stationary over the buoy. Even though we are using a lot of reverse thrust to hold the boat against the wind we still have 2 knots of positive flow over the rudder and, therefore, retain full control. It's worth noting that single screw motorboats with small rudders and big propellers may not enjoy much control by rudder alone, though the principle holds good.

On your final approach, it helps to pick a distant target in transit with the mooring. This will give you something to aim at when the buoy disappears under your bow. Speed of approach can also be difficult to gauge but objects out on your beam can be good indicators.

Fig 2:9 It helps to pick some visual references when making your approach

TIP If you are unsure about the direction of the tide, go and have a look at the buoy first. You will probably be able to see the stream flowing around it or perhaps a pick-up buoy resting on the down tide side.

SECURING TO BUOYS

Mooring buoys come in many shapes and sizes but those reserved for visitors will be large, clearly visible and are often marked as such. They may sometimes have pick-up buoys attached.

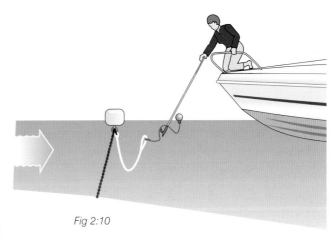

Fig 2:10

If the mooring has a pick-up buoy then approach up-tide with a crew on the foredeck armed with a boathook (Fig 2:10). Remember that the buoy will disappear under your bow as you approach so ask the crew to call out the distances while pointing at it with the hook. Once the boat has been brought to a halt with its bow over the buoy, your crew should sweep under the pick-up buoy's line with the boathook, pull it aboard – ideally over the bow roller or through a fairlead – and secure it to a cleat. You can then relax and put the kettle on.

It's a little more difficult if there isn't a pick-up buoy. Even if you succeed in grabbing the ring in the top of the mooring buoy with your boathook, it is all too easy to lose the battle against the full force of wind and stream. Unfortunately, once a boathook is under load it becomes very difficult to unhook so you may be faced with the decision either to let go of it or follow it overboard.

The easy way to do it is to use a lasso (Fig 2:11). Take both ends of a long and heavy mooring warp and cleat them to the boat with 'figure of eights' – which can always be undone, even under load. Pass the large loop of rope out over your bow roller and then back aboard over the rails. The foredeck crew should now divide the loop of rope into two even handfuls and, when the helmsman brings the boat to a halt, cast the rope out and over the buoy. As the rope settles and sinks, back away from the buoy and the rope will pull tight around the chain beneath the buoy.

Whether by lasso or boathook, if you have to pick up a mooring single-handed, make the initial connection over the stern where you can both drive the boat and reach the buoy. Once you have your temporary connection, take a long warp from the bow to the buoy, release the stern and allow the boat to swing. Finally, pull the bow up to the buoy and secure.

Fig 2:11

WARNING: Never be tempted to make a loop in the end of a warp with a bowline and cast that over a buoy 'rodeo' style. You may not be able to release it later.

MAKING FAST

Remember that a lassoed buoy is not a secure mooring – just a temporary attachment while you get yourself properly sorted.

Once the initial connection is made you can pull both parts of the lasso together, bringing the boat and buoy sufficiently close together to put a proper mooring line through the ring in the top of the buoy. Boats with high freeboards may need to launch a dinghy.

When rigging a more permanent mooring line, pass it through the buoy's ring twice, making a full turn (Fig 2:12). This will allow the rope to partially grip the ring, thus reducing movement and frictional wear. In lively conditions, a single pass through the ring can burn through rapidly.

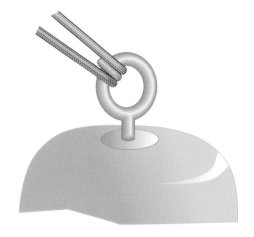

Fig 2:12

Where there may be lots of movement, a prudent skipper will rig a second, slack mooring line just in case the first one fails (Fig 2:13).

Fig 2:13

COMING ALONGSIDE A TIDAL QUAY WALL

Fig 2:14 Not exactly boat friendly! You will need to protect your topsides

The quay shown in the photograph above is typical of many – a masonry wall, protected by timber piles, with steel ladders at regular intervals. Of course, you will need to target one of those ladders so your crew can get on and off at all states of the tide. But the main threat is the timber piles, which present quite a hazard to the sides of small boats. If you hang your fenders in the traditional manner, most will inevitably miss the timber piles leaving your gelcoat liable to damage. It's better, therefore, to hang the fenders in a continuous horizontal row, like a string of sausages (Fig 2:15). You can then be certain that the boat will be protected in the short term.

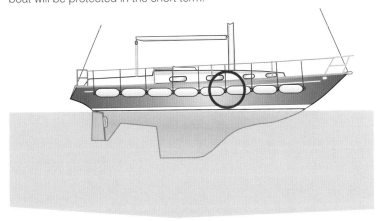

Fig 2:15

Fig 2:16

Fenders can be strung together by passing the lanyard of one fender through the eye on the bottom end of another. You will need an extra line for the last fender

Before going in you should prepare the mooring warps you will need: bow line, bow spring, stern line and stern spring, plus a short mooring warp made ready mid-ships. When you arrive at the ladder position, the short line mid-ships can be slipped around a rung of the ladder and brought back on board. When the line is made fast the boat will be held securely for a few minutes while you sort out the final mooring arrangement. Once the proper mooring system is secure, remember to release the line so that the boat can ride up and down on the tide.

Don't forget the stream. If you are unsure which way it runs take a dummy run first. If, on the approach, you feel your stern trying to overtake your bow, you have chosen the wrong direction. On the other hand, if you feel in control as you slow down you have probably chosen correctly. A good check is to try and turn the bow both ways. If the bow responds you have steerageway.

THE FERRY GLIDE

You can harness the force of the stream to move a boat sideways. The method has been used by ferrymen since the days when they were powered by oars, so the technique is known as the 'Ferry Glide'. Basically if a boat is set at an angle to the stream (Fig 2:17) and is driven slowly forward then the forward vector will combine with the stream vector to produce a sideways movement. If the boat's angle to the stream is reduced then the sideways movement will reduce and if the boat's angle to the stream is increased then the sideways drift will increase. Alternatively if the boat's angle to the stream is held constant but the boat speed is reduced, then the sideways drift will increase, while increasing speed will slow the sideways drift. In practice most helmsmen will use a combination of the two methods. Ferry gliding is an extremely useful technique and many helmsmen will use it to a greater or lesser extent whenever they are operating in a strong stream.

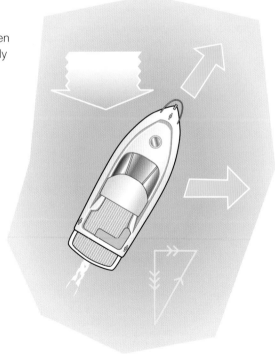

Another fundamental technique, used to keep you on a straight line approach, is the 'transit', steering to keep two convenient objects in line (in transit). The combination of the ferry glide and a transit makes for an extremely powerful tool that will allow you to drive successfully in and out of very tight spots (See Fig 2:18).

Fig 2:17

2

LINES OF APPROACH

Once you have decided which way the tide is flowing and selected a suitable landing point, you need to select the line of approach. Two points should be borne in mind: firstly, which way the stern will kick in reverse and, secondly, for a sailing boat that will pivot around its keel, how much room should be left for the stern to swing.

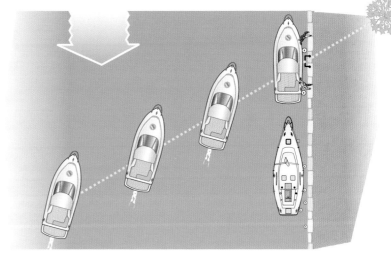

Fig 2:18 *The ladder and the tree provides a handy transit to bring this boat alongside. There is usually a transit to be found in most situations*

In Fig 2:18 the helmsman has selected a good approach angle, about 60° to the wall, and has also chosen a convenient transit. Steering so as to keep his transit points in line, he proceeds directly in, using the current vector to ferry glide towards the wall, maintaining his ability to manoeuvre until the last moment.

It's important not to approach at too shallow an angle. Fig 2:19 shows a helmsman arriving at the wall too early, whereupon he finds he has not left enough room to swing the stern towards the wall, so is unable to swing the bow out. As the boat slows, the effects of the tide take over, pressing her down onto a moored yacht. In these circumstances, there's plenty of scope for expensive damage to all concerned.

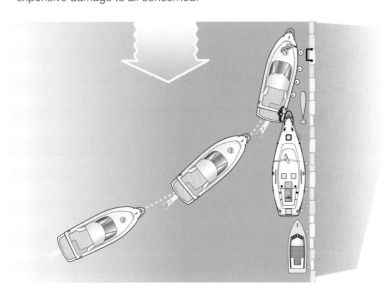

Fig 2:19

In this example a berth has been allocated on a wall deep between two rafts of yachts – another situation where the ferry glide will serve us well. Let's take this step-by-step, below.

1: **The helmsman has selected an appropriate transit, slowed the engine down to just enough to stem the stream, and has set the boat at a good angle to it. The helmsman has decided to use steering with a constant slow engine speed to achieve mooring.**

2: **He finds that he has dropped back on the transit and so steers a little into the tide.**

3: **He is back onto the transit and simply maintains the angle to the tide, moving sideways.**

4: **Now he has advanced against the transit and needs to increase the angle to the tide to drop back onto the transit.**

5: **He has now dropped back onto the transit and is moving quickly sideways towards the ladder.**

6: **Finally, the boat has been 'squared' to the wall and is 'hovering' nicely, allowing the mooring party to secure her to the quay.**

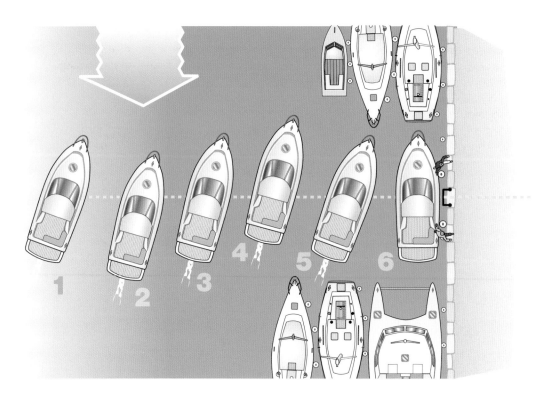

Fig 2:20

LEAVING

Leaving a wall or pontoon is easy as long as you first give the matter proper thought and then take a few minutes to prepare. If your crew let go of all of the lines and you drive forward, your stern will inevitably bump along the wall until you finally get the bow out far enough to achieve some clearance and may seriously damage your boat. If the wind is blowing you 'onshore' – against the quay – you might not get clear at all, plus there's always the chance of leaving your shore crew behind.

Fig 2:21

Let's start with the basics. First have a look at the direction of the current. If the tide is flowing from astern you should reverse, into the tide. If the current is flowing from ahead then you should go out forwards.

Although the principles hold true in either direction, let's say that the stream is flowing from ahead and that we are going out forward. The first job is to re-arrange all of the mooring lines so that they have half turns around whatever they are attached to ashore and so they can all be slipped from onboard – made into 'slip lines'. The whole process of getting your lines ready to let go is known as 'singling up', which we shall return to in more detail later. The lines can, of course, be quite short, as you will only be staying for a few more minutes. Finally, reposition the fenders to protect the boat as you leave.

On slipping, our plan is to arrange for the bow (or stern if the stream is from astern) to point away from the wall by say 30° – more if there are moored boats ahead. Basically we need to drive away at such an angle that we can swing the stern without hitting the wall as we depart.

If there's an offshore wind, we don't need to be too technical. You simply slip the springs and bow line and hold onto the stern line long enough for the bow to blow away from the wall and for the stream to start working on the hull and keel. When the boat is pointing well away from the wall, slip the stern line and, once it is absolutely clear, drive ahead. If you are worried about slipping astern a metre or two (3-6 feet) then make a slipping stern spring the last line to let go.

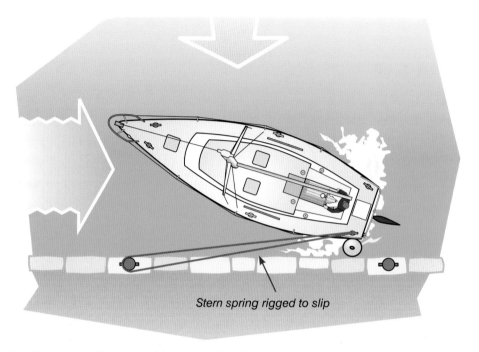

Stern spring rigged to slip

Fig 2:22 Springing off is a powerful technique which allows you to leave, even against a strong onshore wind

Springing off

An onshore wind complicates matters, as it will tend to hold the boat against the wall. This situation calls for a procedure known as 'springing off'. Again, the principle works whether you are leaving bow or stern first, but for now let's stick with going out forward.

We need to rig a stern slip line spring to pull the bow out, but we can single up the other lines to just a bow and stern line. Also put an extra fender on the quarter next to the wall.

■ First engage a little reverse power then slip the stern line.

■ When you are clear to leave, slip the bow line and watch the stern swing towards the wall.

■ As the fendered quarter makes contact with the wall, increase reverse power until the bow has pulled away far enough for the stream to act on the hull and keel and help the bow pull out further.

■ Once you are confident that everything is satisfactory, put the engine into neutral, slip the spring, engage forward gear and drive away.

Other variations on this technique are covered in the OUT OF THE MARINA section.

3 INTO THE MARINA

PLANNING

Marinas can seem daunting. Lots of tight corners, dead ends and very expensive boats full of experienced sailors who have all managed to put their boats in without incident – and who are now going to watch you attempt the same feat. Take heart. You shouldn't be daunted at all. Marinas are designed specifically for the purpose of mooring boats, so what could possibly go wrong? If you do a little bit of planning and apply a couple of basic rules, nothing!

Marinas come in two main types. The first are located on riverbanks. They have long pontoons stretching out from the shore with finger berths either side pointing upstream and downstream. The stream in this type of marina will always be significant, probably strongest on the ebb when the river current will combine with the tidal flow. A kind hearted berthing master will offer you a berth approachable head to tide but, beware, for this won't always be the case.

The second type are those that are either partially or completely enclosed in a basin, so that there are no appreciable streams to worry about. Without a stream to hinder or help you, decisions on your approach angle will probably be decided by the wind direction and your ability to use the boat's momentum to your advantage.

We are approaching a strange marina at the end of a long passage. Our first point of reference should be the Almanac, Pilot Book or Marina Directory, so that we can examine a plan of the marina and get a feel for the way the pontoons are numbered. Depending on the type of marina, we might also want to know what streams to expect. Then there's the matter of whether it's predominantly a visitors' marina, in which case we can choose our own berth in the assigned area – usually well marked – or a residents' marina, where we will have to contact them in advance to make sure there is an available berth.

If we need to call on VHF, it should be on the marina's own working channel – Channel 80 for all UK marinas, or whichever channel is given in the almanac for those elsewhere. Mobile phones are also useful – telephone numbers are given in almanacs – and allow berths to be booked well ahead. We should expect to be allocated a berth by number and also to be advised on the direction of any stream and whether the port or starboard side will be against the finger pontoon.

Next, the boat should be made ready, preparing for any eventuality. Fenders on both sides, bow and stern lines on both sides and, if we are short handed, a line from the mid-ships cleat on both sides. Even the best laid plans can go awry, so it's essential we provide ourselves with the option to change our minds at the last moment – perhaps going in stern first rather than bow first. Having both sides prepared is a very worthwhile precaution.

Lastly we should take a look at the berth from as close as possible before committing ourselves, and then decide on the line of approach. In choosing the correct line we should consider the following three factors in this order of priority:

1   We want the final contact to be into the stream.

2   We want the boat's momentum to carry us onto the berth.

3   If possible, it would be nice to approach heading either directly upwind or downwind.

Mid-ships spring

Before we look at specific berthing strategies, it's worth describing the mid-ships spring – an extremely useful tool, particularly when short-handed. Most finger berths are so short that bow and stern lines alone won't hold a boat in position – it takes a couple of additional spring lines to do that, and they can't be rigged in a hurry.

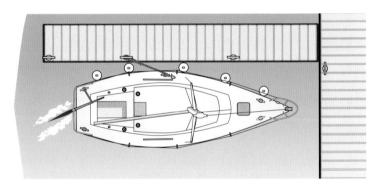

Fig 3:1 Mid-ships spring

However, a mid-ships spring will hold your boat alongside, totally under control, for as long as it takes to get your other mooring lines sorted. Here's how to go about it:

1   Secure the spring to the mid-ships cleat and make a loop in the other end.

2   As the boat comes alongside, a crew member steps ashore and drops the loop over a convenient cleat on the pontoon.

3   Motor gently ahead against the spring, steering the stern in against the pontoon. As long as you keep the power on, the boat will be held in place, even in a weather berth. Motor boats with their pivot points a long way aft may find that a stern line works better.

SITUATION 1: HEAD TO STREAM

This is the ideal situation, with a strong stream giving us plenty of control. Potential problems are few but we must be careful not to let the stream push us too close to the boats and pontoons on our left as we enter – and that means keeping enough clearance for our stern to swing out as we turn. We also don't want to hit the boat to starboard as we push into the berth. Here our momentum should work for us, keeping us away from our neighbour and pushing us onto our berth.

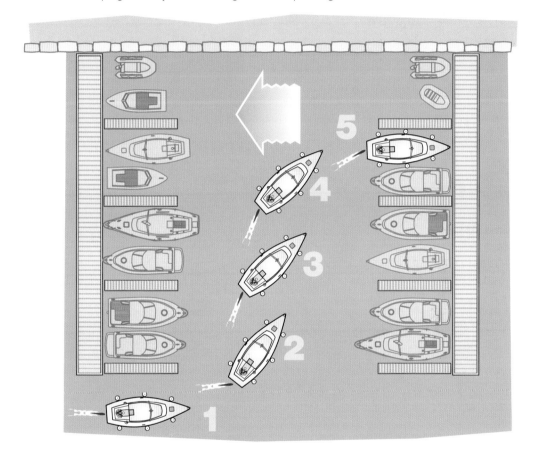

1:   **We have good control so can pause to have a look where we are going. It always helps to appraise a situation rather than just rashly charging in.**

2:   **At this point we are starting to run in, keeping well upstream of the boats on the pontoon to the left.**

3 & 4: **Now we are ferry gliding to port along the centreline between the two pontoons.**

5:   **Finally, we have driven ahead just fast enough to overcome the stream. The boat's momentum pushes us onto the finger berth and away from the boat moored to starboard.**

SITUATION 2: HEAD TO STREAM, TURN FIRST

There are two problems in this situation. As in the previous situation, we mustn't allow the stream to push us down onto the boats on the other pontoon, so we will need to stay near the centre line of the fairway. But, this time, if we go for the direct approach then the boat's momentum will pull us away from our berth. So, to make momentum work in our favour, we need to approach the berth from the other direction – from inside the marina. There are always at least two ways of doing this, one of which would be to reverse down the fairway, past our berth, and then motor forward for the final approach. But our helm has decided to drive forwards into the marina, then turn through the stream using our slow speed turning technique to make the final approach from there.

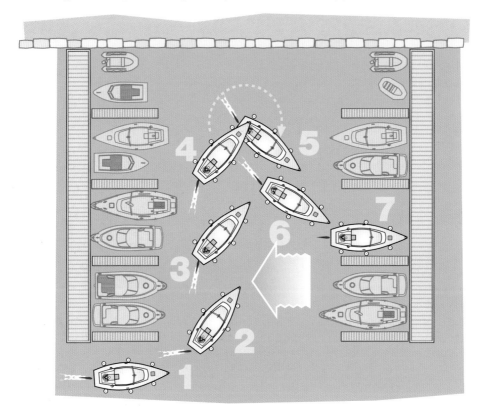

1: **We pause to have a look at the situation.**

2 & 3: **Now we are ferry gliding nicely between the pontoons, taking care to stay well clear of the boats downstream.**

4: **At this point we are making our slow speed turn through the stream – see page 17 for details of this manoeuvre.**

5 & 6: **We are ferry gliding back almost the way we came in.**

7: **Having motored into the berth, we allow the momentum to place us nicely alongside.**

SITUATION 3: DOWNSTREAM

Here we are faced with one of the most awkward situations. Downstream into a bay with a closed end and probably another boat close alongside. If we go in head first with a single screw sailboat and have to pull out in a hurry, we would be fighting a strong stream with our relatively ineffective reverse gear and lots of prop walk – not a great idea. The solution is to reverse into the berth so we can retain the maximum control.

1: **As usual we pause for that all important look.**

2, 3 & 4: **Having decided that there's enough stream to ferry glide effectively, we do exactly that, ferry gliding to starboard along the centreline between the pontoons.**

5 & 6: **Here we can hover head to stream and slowly reduce revs until we start to drop back with the stream. If we have over-estimated the stream, we may need to use reverse to drop down into the bay. That part of the movement feels very uncomfortable as we lose steerage for a moment or two but once we are deep in the bay we can swing the rudder to port and give a good burst of forward power – position 6. That burst gives us immediate steerageway and pulls the bow out from the finger, all at the same time. We can then manoeuvre gently alongside with just enough power to buck the stream.**

If the stream had been weaker, we could have simply reversed all the way in, allowing the boat's momentum to throw us out against the finger, knowing that at any time we could regain good slow speed control by going forward.

Motorboats, including steerable drive boats will be better off going in head first, downstream, then using their excellent reverse capability to reverse alongside into the stream.

SITUATION 4: DOWNSTREAM, STOP AND REVERSE

In this situation we again have a downstream approach, but we've decided that the stream is weak and ferry gliding unnecessary. However, we want our final landing to be into stream and have the boat's momentum to work for us. So we will motor forward deep into the marina, where the stream will be further reduced and then, taking a long run up, will reverse towards our berth. The potential problem is being pushed downstream onto the vessels and pontoons on our starboard side so, to avoid that, we will stay on the upstream side of the fairway centreline and swing our stern into the berth sharply and late.

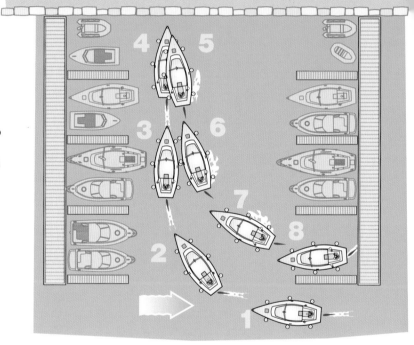

1, 2 & 3: **First we motor into the marina taking care that we are not being set down onto the berths to starboard.**

4, 5: **Here we go into reverse and start to retrace our steps, gaining control and improving our feel for the handling as we go. We are taking care to stay on the high side of the centreline between the pontoons.**

6: **Approaching the berth, we start to steer the stern into the bay.**

7: **Our momentum is already pushing us out of our turning circle and we start to accelerate as the stream adds to our boat speed. No need to worry because…**

8: **… as we come alongside, a good burst of forward power with the rudder already turned to port both stops us in our tracks and swings the bow towards the finger. With the stream now pouring past our rudder we can enjoy lots of slow speed control to place the boat gently on the finger berth.**

Again, twin and single engined motorboats, with their excellent reverse capability, will prefer to drive forwards into a downstream berth, essentially hanging the boats on their propellers/outdrives as they drop into the bay. But remember the boats will be operating in reverse as soon as they slow down and as they manoeuvre alongside.

SITUATION 5: STILL WATER, LEEWARD FINGER BERTH

We are now entering a marina with no appreciable stream, but with a strong breeze to push us onto our allocated berth. We have decided that we can operate almost head to wind at such a slow speed that momentum can be ignored while using the wind to our advantage. The potential problem is that we could be blown onto the end of the finger before we are properly in the berth. To avoid this we need to keep the whole boat to windward of an imaginary extension of the berth's edge throughout the final stages of the approach.

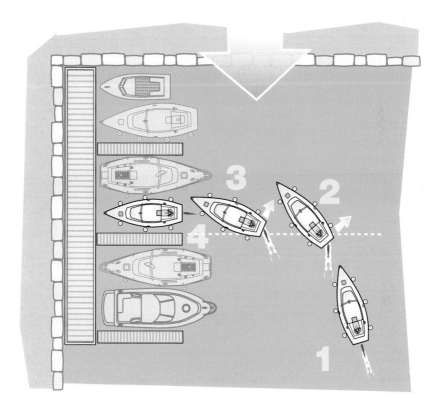

1: **We are coasting in neutral, allowing the boat to slow while keeping as well clear of the berths to port as possible.**

2: **The boat stalls, so we apply port rudder with a short burst of forward power. The bow is now pivoting towards the berth.**

3: **We notice that our stern hasn't yet cleared an imaginary extension of the finger berth's edge, so we motor forward a couple of metres (6.6 feet) until it does.**

4: **A little more port rudder and another nudge forward so that the bow, now helped by the wind, pivots towards the berth. We can now drive into the slot, finally applying enough reverse to stop the boat while the wind pushes us gently alongside.**

SITUATION 6: WINDWARD FINGER BERTH

We are in the same marina but this time we have been allocated a windward berth, starboard side-to. We know that as we slow the boat to pick up the mooring, the wind will push us away from the berth, so we need to be quite positive in our approach, maximising the effect of momentum. There may not be enough time for more than one person to get off the boat before the wind blows us away, so we have decided to use our single line mid-ships spring technique (page 30).

1: **We approach the berth at a couple of knots, keeping the bow up into the wind as far as possible.**

2: **Now in neutral, our speed is dropping slowly and we are steering first at the end of the finger and then running the bow down the finger's edge so that the widest part of the boat is steered alongside. As it comes within reach our crew drops the pre-made loop in the end of our single mooring line over the first cleat on the end of the finger.**

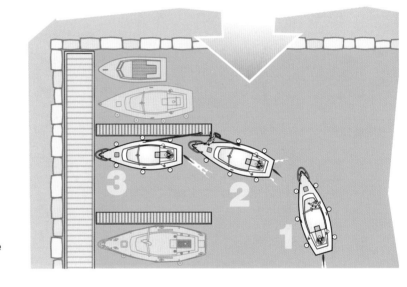

3: **The mooring line becomes taut and we apply forward thrust while steering the boat's stern in towards the finger. The boat is now totally under control and we can set about completing the mooring.**

Remember that the single line is fixed at a point mid-ships, opposite our pivot point so we can still steer the boat effectively while we push against the line. A motorboat's pivot point is much nearer the stern, so motor boats can use a stern line to the same effect.

Note that we've prepared fenders on our port side for this manoeuvre. This gives us an escape route. If we fail to pick up the mooring or if the wind is too strong and we don't get close enough to our finger then we can stop the boat with a good burst astern and allow the wind to push us gently down on to the leeward finger (or a neighbouring boat if there is one). This is a much safer solution than attempting to reverse out to start the manoeuvre again.

SITUATION 7: WINDWARD FINGER BERTH WITH STREAM UNDER THE PONTOON

This situation shows an elegant solution to an awkward problem. It's a technique that will get you out of trouble in quite extreme conditions. Imagine we have entered a busy harbour with both the stream and wind conspiring to keep you off your allocated starboard side-to berth. A traditional approach simply won't allow you enough time alongside to get crew and lines ashore, because as soon as you turn broadside to the wind and stream they will push you away from the pontoon. Fortunately, there's a way round this problem.

1: **Motoring gently forward, we carefully position the bow over the pontoon cleat that will end up just astern of the yacht when moored. Our crew has prepared a mid-ships spring on the starboard side (see page 30) and run it forward to the starboard bow, outside all rigging, guardwires and rails. The spring has a pre-made loop in the end, which is dropped over the cleat. We now put the engine in neutral and wait for nature to take charge.**

2: **The boat will drop back until the spring becomes taut and will hang there, more or less broadside to the wind and stream.**

3: **The final part of the manoeuvre involves powering forward against the spring, steering to keep the boat parallel with the pontoon.**

4: **Given enough thrust, the boat will push up alongside the pontoon and we can hold it there while the crew step ashore and complete the mooring.**

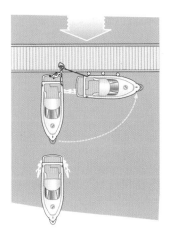

If performing this manoeuvre single-handed, make the initial approach in reverse so you will be on hand, both to drive the boat and to handle the spring over the stern.

Twin engine vessels will certainly prefer to reverse towards their chosen stern pontoon cleat, this time dropping a prepared stern line over it. Powering forward on their outside engine will then push them onto their berth.

Single engine, steerable drive boats can also use a stern line and reverse approach or use a long bow line and steer into it like this:

1, 2: Our RIB driver noses up to the pontoon, and drops a pre-prepared loop in the end of his painter over the cleat.

2, 3: After allowing the RIB to settle back with the wind and stream, he then applies full starboard lock and forward gear and pushes against the painter until alongside the pontoon.

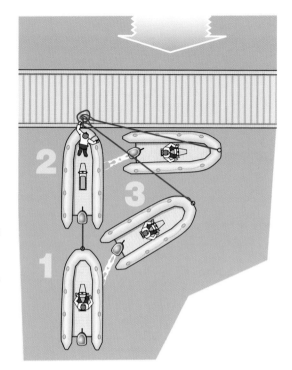

GENERAL ADVICE

Most marinas have nice long finger berths, that are wide, safe, with ample strong cleats arranged along their length. But some aren't. In my years as a training skipper I've encountered fingers that are far too short for the boats they accommodate, some without cleats, just metal loops on the end, some that submerge when more than one adult steps on and many that are very slippery particularly after rain. I have had two relatively inexperienced crew jump enthusiastically ashore and disappear through the timber decking, and more than a couple who have skidded on the finger and fallen into the water on the other side. They have usually been considerate enough to hang on to their mooring lines, but it doesn't provide for a dignified end to a successful manoeuvre. So be careful – especially at the end of a rough passage or a night passage. Also make sure that all of your crew have disconnected their harnesses before they attempt to step ashore.

Many less experienced helmsmen fail to stop when they bring their boats alongside, relying on the mooring party to bring the boat to a halt. Don't just stare ahead when you come alongside but pay attention to the pontoon or wall alongside you. You will then be able to see immediately whether you are still moving forward or astern.

TIP If this is your permanent berth, establish some visual references to help you the next time you moor up. With the boat properly moored, stand at your normal steering position and note where the pontoon appears to intersect the gunwale and where the end of the finger lies relative to your boat. When next you enter the berth you will know exactly where to stop your boat so it is correctly positioned.

4 OUT OF THE MARINA

GETTING READY TO GO

In could be said that this section should have come first, since leaving a finger berth is often the first manoeuvre one might have to carry out – probably before we have had a chance to become familiar with the boat's particular characteristics. So don't be rushed into a hasty departure. Take time to thoroughly assess all of the outside influences that might try to take control of the boat and decide how best to deal with each. Look into the water to see how the stream is affecting your particular berth. Look at your wind indicator, or those on neighbouring boats to decide which way it will try to blow you once you have slipped. Establish the direction your stern will kick when you apply astern power (see page 11). Imagine how all these factors will affect your ability to leave.

Singling up

Next, take time to prepare thoroughly for departure. Adjust all of the mooring lines so that they are converted into slip lines – that's to say, lines attached to the boat with half turns around the pontoon cleats and then returned on board. Lines currently serving no useful purpose – for instance a spring intended to work with the stream running in the other direction – can be removed. We call

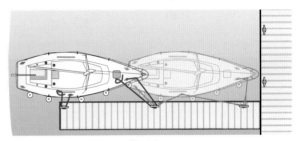

Fig 4:1

the process 'singling up' and, if you start with a spare line and adjust each mooring line in turn, you won't lose control of the boat. It might seem long winded but taking the time to single up properly will ensure that you don't leave anybody behind, have any crew injure themselves while trying to leap aboard at the last moment and also that the helm stays in control of the whole manoeuvre.

SOME GENERAL WARNINGS

Any line that you want to slip from onboard must be plain ended. A knot or loop in the end is sure to catch on the pontoon cleat at the worst possible moment. Also encourage your crew to slip by simply pulling the line back aboard. Trying to flick the line off the pontoon cleat will often put an extra turn around the cleat's tang, locking the rope, again, just when you need it to run free.

It is always worth putting out some fenders on the side away from the pontoon, before slipping. If you have enough available crew, designate one of them as a 'wandering fender', whose job is to keep a look out all the way around the boat and place the fender (not themselves) between the boat and anything else you may come in contact with.

Finally, if it does all start to go wrong, don't attempt a dramatic recovery which might make matters worse. Simply take the way off the boat and let her settle gently against whatever it is you're in danger of hitting. This way, you can then work out how to extricate yourself gently, with the only damage being to your ego.

Now let's look at some common situations. A sailing yacht is shown in the first few examples, but for these particular circumstances the principles apply to all boat types. We will assume that you have to leave the berth in reverse, because that's most likely and probably more awkward.

In marinas where there's a strong stream, we need to avoid driving downstream while still in the narrow fairways. The danger is that the stream could sweep us down onto other moored yachts before we are able to gather way. Here's how it can happen.

Upstream exit

Our helmsman has slipped and, with lots of stream running from astern, enjoys good slow speed control as he reverses as far upstream as he can. At position 2 he then applies lots of port rudder and gives a good burst ahead to turn the boat towards the exit.

Unfortunately, he has underestimated the effect of the stream and is pushed down onto the moored boats.

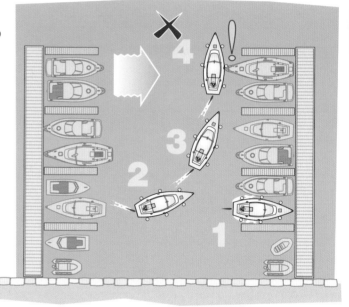

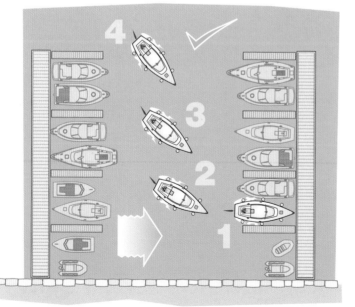

Next time our intrepid helmsman decides to use the stream to his advantage and stays in reverse, ferry gliding towards the exit under perfect control while staying on the upstream side of the fairway.

Downstream exit

Inspired by his success, he later decides to motor out in reverse again. Unfortunately, he fails to notice that the tide has turned and his exit is now downstream. This time he is swept down onto the boats on the other side of the fairway.

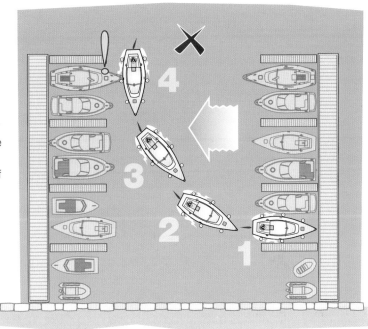

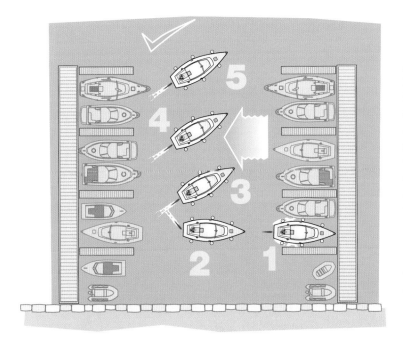

Having finally learned his lesson, our helmsman takes the stream into account and slips out of his berth using the minimum of reverse thrust. Once his bow is clear, he applies full port rudder and a short burst of forward drive (position 2). His bow pivots over to the left and using low revs our helm is able to ferry glide out of the marina under perfect control.

The moral to take from both of these scenarios is that we should use the current, not fight it, and always apply the first golden rule, namely: When manoeuvring at slow speed, steer into the stream.

USING WARPS TO ADVANTAGE

Let's look at some ways that we can make our mooring lines (warps) work for us. Not all of these techniques work well for all boat shapes and types, but here's a selection and you can choose those that will work for you.

We have already looked at singling up (page 39) but, while you are about it, you might be able to move your boat to a more advantageous position if there's room. That way, you are then half way out of the berth before you slip, with less opportunity for things to go wrong.

We usually want to point our boats away from the pontoon before driving away. Creating a little bit of distance between the boat and the pontoon gives us the opportunity to swing the stern both ways, improving our ability to manoeuvre. If we are leaving in

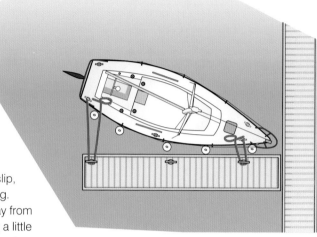

Fig 4:2 Adjusting your lines can make it much easier to leave

reverse and our boat has a rounded hull shape, we can simply pull in on the bow line and ease the stern line before slipping, pointing the stern away from the pontoon and, maybe, even into the wind (Fig 4:2).

Way back (on page 28) we described a boat springing off a wall in order to leave bow first. Of course, the same technique can be applied when leaving stern first (Fig 4:3). Like this:

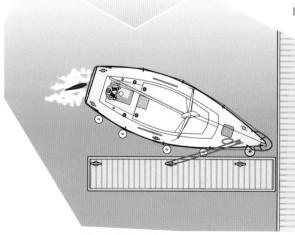

Fig 4:3 With a brisk onshore wind you might need to spring off

■ Rig a slipping bow spring from the boat's bow to the middle pontoon cleat and return it to the bow. Put a fender as far forward as possible.

■ As you can then motor gently forward, slip the bow and stern lines but hold tight the spring. Now increase the forward thrust and steer the stern away from the pontoon.

■ When you have enough clearance select neutral, slip the spring, and when you are sure that there are no snags drive away astern.

This solution shown in Fig 4:4 can be applied in even more extreme circumstances. It's time to leave, but we are deep in the marina with a strong wind blowing us onto our berth.

■ Again, rig a nice long slipping bow spring with plenty of fenders near to the bow.

■ Motoring forward against the spring, we push the bow into contact with the pontoon and, with steadily increased revs, steer the stern up into the wind.

■ With stern dead to wind, we can select neutral, slip the spring and – after checking for snags – reverse away.

Even a single screw boat will steer easily against the wind in reverse, since the bow will 'weather vane' behind the propeller. If instead we had a stream running through the marina from right to left, we would have had to use a stern spring to point the bow away from the wall in order that we could take off into the stream. The procedure would go as follows:

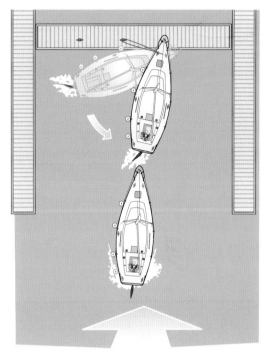

Fig 4:4

■ A slipping stern spring is rigged from the port quarter, with plenty of fenders there to protect the hull.

■ You then apply steady power in reverse. Once the quarter has made contact with the wall, increase the power to full and watch the bow pull away. Your rudder, of course is ineffective at this stage since the prop thrust is working forward, away from it, so springing off by the stern is not as effective as springing by the bow.

■ Hopefully the stream will begin to assist the movement away from the wall but, as you sense that the turn is stalling, put the engine in neutral, allow the boat to surge forward, slip the spring, then apply full starboard rudder and a couple of bursts of forward power to push the bow up into the wind.

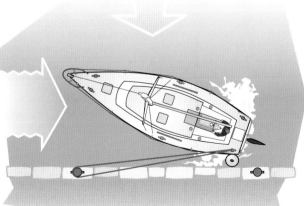

Fig 4:5 Here we use the stream to push the bow round

TAMING THE PROP WALK EFFECT

We know that you get maximum prop walk when you go astern from a standstill – exactly the situation when you reverse out of a finger berth. Sometimes this is an advantage but other times it's not. If prop walk is a nuisance, you can often use dragged warps to counteract its action.

Dragging entails letting go of one end of a slip line then letting the movement of the boat pull the line past the pontoon cleat. The friction on the line may be enough to induce a turn in a desired direction or stop the boat turning the other way as a result of prop walk – or, indeed, wind action.

For instance, let's say that we are moored 'starboard side-to' on a finger berth and want to slip out straight astern. If the boat normally kicks to port in reverse then, by dragging the stern line as we go backwards, the pull on the starboard quarter might be enough to stop the stern kicking to port, with the result that we should be able to steer backwards in a straight line (Fig 4:6).

If, on the other hand, our boat normally kicks to starboard, we could drag the bow line. Stopping the bow swinging to port will stop the stern swinging to starboard, producing the same result (Fig 4:7).

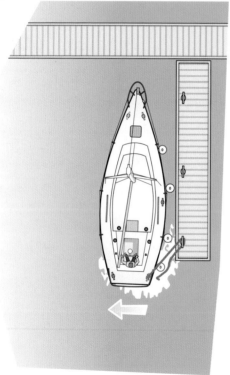

Fig 4:6 Dragging a mooring line from the stern helps reduce a kick to port .....

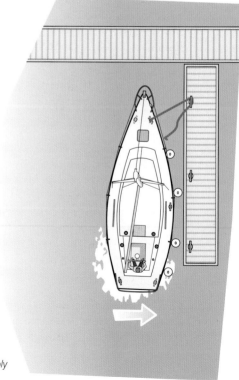

Fig 4:7 ..... while dragging a line from the bow will do the same for a kick to starboard. Obviously if the boat was port side to, the opposites would apply

WIND OFF THE PONTOON

Good use of warps to maintain control as we gather way astern is vital when the wind is blowing us off of our berth – especially if there's a neighbouring boat alongside. If we just slip and go, we stand a good chance of being driven onto our neighbour before we have a chance to gather steerageway. Handily, we can use our mooring warps to avoid such an unfortunate incident.

The boat type with the worst handling characteristics for marina work is the long keeled sailing yacht, so we will use that as an example. But all boat types can make good use of this technique. For instance, although in theory a twin screw motor yacht with bow thrusters has lots of handling advantages, its tremendous windage can make things very difficult in a crosswind.

So, back to the example. We want to back out of the berth and swing our stern to starboard so that we can drive forwards out of the marina, but we have a Force 5 wind pushing us off of the pontoon and our boat kicks to port when driving astern. We are set up to go with a stern line, bow line and bow spring all rigged to slip.

Then:

1: As we start to reverse we ease out the bow and stern lines simultaneously while taking in the slack in the bow spring (not shown), essentially using the reverse thrust and the short lines to keep the boat up against the pontoon.

2: When the bow reaches the end pontoon cleat, the bow line is released and the bow spring is eased out.

3: Once our bow has cleared the stern of our neighbour, the bow spring is released and the stern line held tight. Our stern then turns to starboard while our bow swings quickly to port.

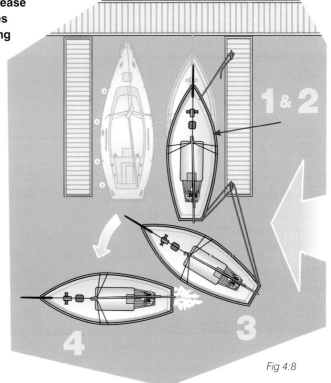

Fig 4:8

4: As soon as we are pointing in the right direction, the stern line is released and we can drive comfortably ahead. Throughout the operation the stern line prevented prop walk from pulling the stern to port.

GALE FROM AHEAD

Now we want to reverse our awkward long keeler out of the same berth, but this time with a full gale blowing from ahead. Again, if we just slip and go, our bow could be blown onto our neighbour before we have a chance to gather stern way. Even if we made it out of the berth, the wind could spin the boat and leave us out of control in the narrow fairway. So here's a method for using mooring warps to tame the wind and make the boat do what we want it to.

Basically the wind will blow the boat right out of the berth but we must prevent the bow blowing away too early, and also want the stern to swing to starboard so that we can drive forwards out of the marina. So first we will set up the boat with a bow line and bow spring, set to slip, and also a mid-ship spring around the end pontoon cleat, also set to slip.

Then:

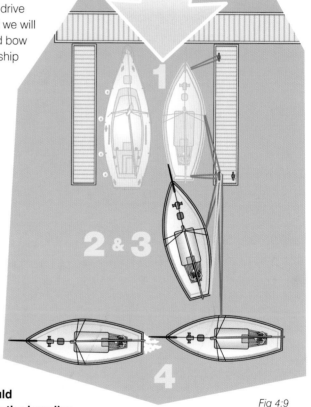

1: **When we are ready to start, we slip the stern line and, while pulling in on the mid-ships and the bow spring, ease out the bow line so that the boat starts to move backwards.**

2: **As our mid-ships cleat moves past the end pontoon cleat, we start to ease the mid-ships spring while still pulling in on the bow spring and easing the bow line.**

3: **As the bow passes the end of the pontoon, we should ease the bow spring and slip the bow line.**

Fig 4:9

4: **Once we are sure that our bow can swing to port, clear of our neighbour's stern, we can slip the bow spring while holding tight to the mid-ships spring. Our bow must now swing to port until the boat is held at right angles to the wind. Wait at this point until all is settled then simply slip the mid-ships spring and drive away forwards.**

Some of the techniques described in this section seem long winded and hard work, but the saying 'if something can go wrong it will' applies particularly to boats, so digging out and rigging a couple of extra warps to ensure a sweet exit in difficult conditions is well worth the effort.

5 BOAT TYPES AND THEIR LIMITATIONS

arlier, we discussed the handling characteristics of various boat types. Having now covered basic manoeuvres it would be helpful to look again at their limitations and special problems and consider how we can best deal with them. Inevitably, these are broad categories and the distinction between them might be somewhat blurred.

Sailing cruiser – fin or twin keeled

With the propeller well aft and close to the rudder, prop thrust is excellent. These can be pivoted around their keels quite easily, at very slow speed using bursts of drive. The pivot point is close to the mid-length of each boat, so forward control is very good. Mid-ships springs work

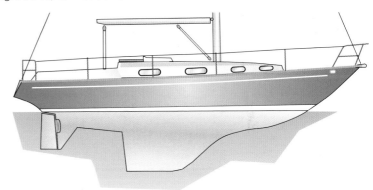

Fig 5:1 Sailing cruiser

well, but you must take care to allow room for your stern to swing when manoeuvring. Without the benefit of prop thrust, reversing is definitely not as positive, but their rudders are relative large, so reverse handling improves with a little bit of speed. Having the propeller so far aft means, of course, that the effect of prop walk when going astern is increased, but we have seen that prop walk can be used to our advantage once its potential is understood.

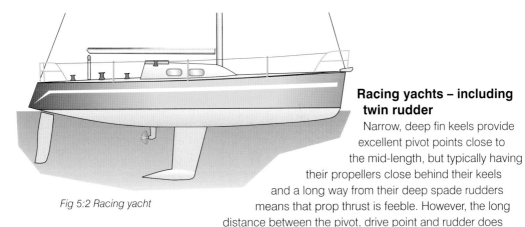

Fig 5:2 Racing yacht

Racing yachts – including twin rudder

Narrow, deep fin keels provide excellent pivot points close to the mid-length, but typically having their propellers close behind their keels and a long way from their deep spade rudders means that prop thrust is feeble. However, the long distance between the pivot, drive point and rudder does mean that these boats will spin easily with only a little bit of forward speed. With the propeller so close to mid-length, prop walk is minimal and can probably be discounted. But you must still allow room for their sterns to swing. Mid-ships springs are very effective as 'arrester wires' or to drive the boats onto weather berths. The folding or feathering propellers employed on these boats may take a moment to open, particularly when going astern, so beware of a delayed braking effect.

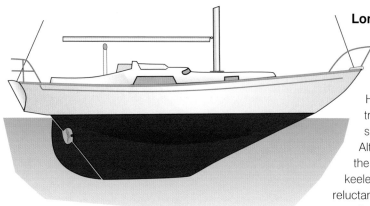

Long keeled sailing yachts

The long keel underwater profile gives superb directional stability but tight turns are impossible. Hardly surprisingly, this traditional type isn't well suited for modern marinas. Although they will respond to the same techniques as the fin keeled boat, they will do so more reluctantly, therefore skippers need to use all of the warping techniques that we have described and more. Old fashioned designs need old fashioned techniques like 'clubbing' the anchor – that is dragging an anchor on a short warp over the sea bed, either to hold a bow up into the stream or wind, or to keep the bow in line behind a reversing propeller.

Fig 5:3 Long keel yacht

Single screw motorboats

This type will have a powerful fixed propeller but a relatively small rudder. At slow speeds prop thrust in short bursts can be used to great effect when manoeuvring forward, and prop walk

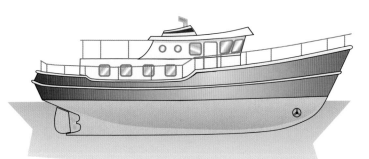

Fig 5:4 Bow thrusters are really useful on boats of this type

should be quite effective when going astern. However, the small rudder will probably make steering in reverse quite difficult. These boats will 'feather' downstream of their propeller or 'weathervane' downwind very well and this characteristic should be exploited. For example a skipper will probably prefer to drop into those downstream dead ends bow first, then relying on his powerful propeller to drag him back out in a straight line. With a pivot point a long way aft these boats may make use of a stern line as an arrester, or as a means of pushing up onto a weather berth. Pushing against a bow line and using their excellent prop thrust to kick the stern towards a pontoon or wall works very well, as long as there's good enough access to the foredeck to handle the line.

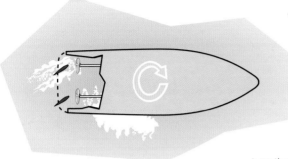

Fig 5:5 *Twin screws*

Twin engine boats

Meaning twin screw diesel yachts, large twin outdrive motorboats, catamarans or any other vessel that has two engines, one on each side of the boat, that can be operated independently. In close quarter manoeuvring, they can centre their helms and turn using combinations of forward and reverse drive on the two engines to turn the boat. At speed, they steer normally. None of these boat types have much grip in the water so they will pivot around a point pretty much between the two propellers. That same lack of grip, however, does leave them at the mercy of cross winds. Some of the larger planing motor yachts with their high superstructures have almost as much windage as a sailing yacht under full sail!

Steerable drive boats

Both at cruising speed and when slow speed manoeuvring, outboard engine and outdrive motorboats steer dynamically by means of directing the thrust from their propellers or drive units. If the engines are put into neutral they will simply drift. With pivot points just forward of their drive units, they are very manoeuvrable in close quarters,

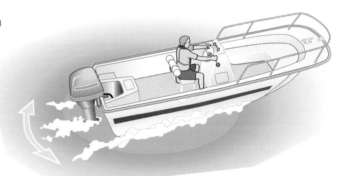

Fig 5:6 *Steerable drive boats, whether outboard or outdrive powered, are all handled in much the same way*

using short bursts of power to change direction. But you have be very quick turning the helm from one side to the other – it can be hard work.

It's often easier to reverse into tight spots since the hulls will 'follow' the drive unit quite well. Going into downstream, or downwind dead ends, however, they usually prefer to go in bow first, allowing the boat to hang on the propeller, finally using their excellent reverse characteristic to pull their sterns onto a pontoon.

Outboard variations

The way that outboard engines are mounted varies considerably. On RIBs and small powerboats they can be singles or twins but either way they act together and operate as steerable drives. On small displacement boats – including sailboats – they can be transom mounted and will be either steerable or fixed, in which case the boat is steered by rudder. Outboards mounted in that fashion do not direct any thrust at their rudders so the boats have to be moving to achieve steerage way. Some outboards sit in a 'well' in front of the rudder, and then take on the handling traits of a single screw displacement boat.

6 ROPES, KNOTS, CLEATS & BOLLARDS

ROPES

All ropes stretch, but some much more than others. Sometimes, stretch is an advantage but more often it's a curse. For running rigging – such as halyards, sheets and guys – the less stretch the better, whereas for mooring and anchor warps, some elasticity helps absorb the shock loads of a boat surging back and forth. The way ropes are constructed also has some bearing on stretch resistance, but the main factor is the type of material they are made from. Let's briefly review the options.

Polyester: A relatively strong and low-stretch material with good wear resistance – by far the most popular choice for running rigging. Various forms of construction are available but the commonest is 'braid on braid' where both the core and the outer covering are braided.

HMPE (High Modulus Polyethylene): A high tech material commonly sold under the brand names Dyneema or Spectra. HMPE ropes are stronger and have lower stretch than polyester and are gaining ground, particularly for use as halyards. Their strength lies solely in their loosely braided inner core. The covers are usually polyester and are there to resist wear.

Nylon: A strong and stretchy rope intended almost exclusively for anchor warps and mooring lines. Construction is usually traditional three-strand but a useful form is a loose eight-plait. Nylon tends to stiffen with age but still retains its strength.

Polypropylene: A light, buoyant rope about the same strength as polyester. Its buoyancy makes it the first choice for liferaft and danbuoy tethers and for heaving lines. Degrades in sunlight, though there have been technical improvements in this regard.

Fig 6:1 8-plait rope

Fig 6:2 Braided rope

Fig 6:3 Three-strand rope

For mooring lines, the form of construction is less important than the material used

CLEATS AND BOLLARDS

Cleats are simple but clever devices for securing a rope quickly. But they must be used correctly – in such a manner that the rope can be released, even when under load. The rope is secured by winding it around the cleat in a series of 'figure of eights' ending with the tail of the rope on top. If the loaded part of the rope traps the turns beneath it, then the rope can't be released (Fig 6:4). The load end of the rope should lead to the cleat with an open angle (Fig 6:5), so that the second turn doesn't jam the first making the release difficult. Three or four figures of eight should be enough to secure a rope but if the rope is particularly slippery you may decide to make a final half hitch on one tang.

Double bollards can also have ropes temporarily secured to them with figures of eight but they are really designed to receive and hold a loop or a half turn from a warp that is singled up ready for slipping. If more than one warp is using the same bollard or cleat with figures of eight then all must be cast off in order to release one. Single bollards, of course, will only receive loops or slip lines.

Bollards and pontoon cleats often have to accommodate more than one mooring line and this is not a problem if we all use loops. To make it possible for any loop to be released without first letting go of the other, each loop should be 'dipped' below the others before it's dropped over (Fig 6:6).

Fig 6:4

Fig 6:5

Fig 6:6

KNOTS

A handful of simple knots will cope with almost every eventuality. Those shown here are the most useful. (See G63 RYA Knots, Splices and Ropework Handbook)

Figure of eight

This is used as a 'stopper' knot to prevent the end of a rope from escaping through a block or sheave. A common use would be the end of a halyard to prevent the end disappearing into the mast

Bowline

By far the best way to form an eye in a rope, and easily untied even after working under load. There are a number of methods of tying a Bowline but the knot's simple construction can be seen from the drawing

Reef Knot

'Right over left and under, left over right and under' is the usual way to tie this knot. If the knot looks twisted rather than lying flat, as shown here, then you have tied a Granny Knot by mistake

Sheet Bend

Not really a knot at all but a 'bend' used for 'bending' two ropes together. The Double Sheet Bend has the rope taken twice around the eye and is more secure than the single

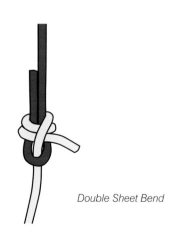

Double Sheet Bend

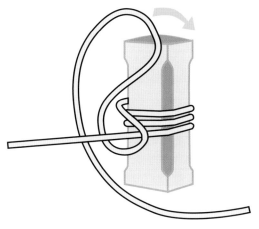

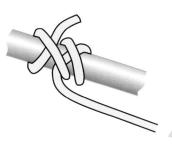

Rolling Hitch

Similar to a Clove Hitch but with an extra locking hitch on one side. The Rolling Hitch is intended to withstand an oblique load without slipping - the load being applied on the same side as the extra turn

Tugboat Hitch

Not a common hitch by any means but a great way to attach a towline to a bollard or Samson post. For simplicity's sake it's not shown here fully completed. In reality the end of the rope would be taken around the back of the bollard and another loop dropped on from the other side. This sequence can be repeated until you are satisfied that all is secure. The tugboat hitch is safe and easy to release under load

Round Turn

The Round Turn and Two Half Hitches is an extremely useful knot with many uses. It can be undone under load so it is ideal for towing or perhaps securing your dinghy painter

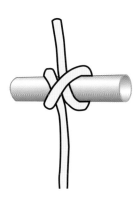

Clove Hitch

This is the preferred method to attach fender lanyards to a guardwire. It must look like it is shown here, otherwise it could be a 'Cow' Hitch which is considerably less secure

7 MOORINGS

ALONGSIDE A TIDAL QUAY

You have brought your boat gently alongside the quay, and secured her temporarily with a line from mid-ships around a rung of the ladder, but the final mooring arrangement must allow for the vertical movement of the boat as she rises and falls with the tide. But, although the boat must be free to move vertically, you need her to stay in place alongside – not least because the crew may want to use the ladder at any state of the tide. To accomplish this you will need four separate mooring warps. Starting from forward:

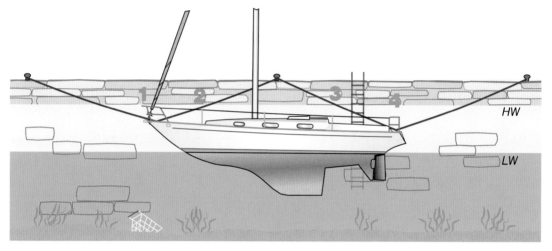

Fig 7:1 Lying alongside a tidal wall presents no problems if you do it correctly

1: **The bow line runs from the boat's bow to the wall ahead of the yacht, and will prevent the bow from swinging away from the wall.**

2: **The bow spring runs from the boat's bow back along the wall, and will stop the boat from surging forward.**

3: **The stern spring, will run from the boat's stern forward to the wall and will stop the boat from surging backwards.**

4: **Lastly, the stern line, will run from the yacht's stern back along the wall and will prevent the stern from swinging away from the wall.**

To decide how long the warps need to be, first take a look at the range of the tide – meaning the amount it will rise and fall on that day at your location. An almanac is the best source for that information. Then multiply the range by three and make that the minimum length of any of the mooring lines. Now you can pull all the warps fairly tight, safe in the knowledge that the boat will rise and fall, keeping station on the ladder, but not dangling from the wall.

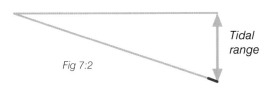

Fig 7:2

Tidal range

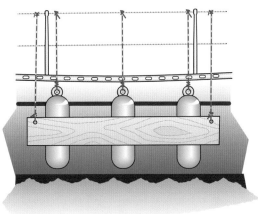

Figure 7:2 shows a 3:1 ratio triangle. The red section on the hypotenuse shows how little extra rope length is needed as the tide falls. Of course a ratio of four or five to one would be even better, but that might not be practicable against a crowded quay. With the boat fully secured it's time to sort out the fenders. Set pairs of fenders near each pile and span them with a fender board (Fig 7:3). Attach the fender board to the boat, so that it goes up and down with you, sliding nicely against the timber pile.

Fig 7:3

NON-TIDAL MOORINGS AND FLOATING PONTOONS

The non-tidal situation is much easier. We still need four warps: a bow line to stop the bow from swinging away, a stern line to do the same job aft, and two springs to stop the boat from surging backwards and forwards. But, at least, both boat and pontoon float up and down with any tide, so we don't have to worry about the length of the warps. Personally I like the springs to run from the centre pontoon cleat to the ends of the boat. That keeps all of the control points together, and leaves the middle of the boat, where people step aboard, free of clutter. Incidentally, it's considered courteous to have all loose ends of the warps on your boat, not on the pontoon where others could trip over them.

The tension on the warps should be adjusted carefully. Many moorings are subject to swell set up by larger commercial craft, so leave your bow and stern lines relatively slack so that they don't snatch as the boat rocks. The springs can be pulled relatively tight so that the boat stays on station.

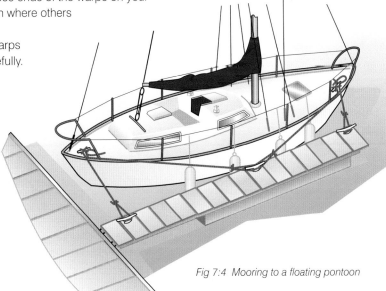

Fig 7:4 Mooring to a floating pontoon

TROT MOORINGS

Trots are pairs of piles or buoys arranged in rows for boats to moor between, fore and aft. They are found in rivers and harbours with tidal streams running through them and where there's not enough room for the boats to swing with the tides. The moorings should be aligned with the stream so the boats will either be bow or stern on to the stream, depending on whether it's flooding or ebbing.

For a single screw boat, picking up a Trot mooring is best done using a running stern line. Other types would probably choose running bow lines. But whether you have a single screw, twin engine, or steerable drive the first thing to do is note the direction of both stream and wind. The first, of course, should be obvious, but the wind could be coming from anywhere.

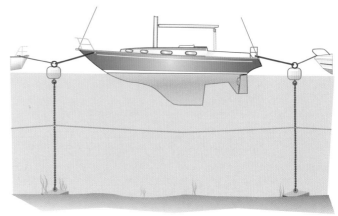

Fig 7:5 Trot buoys - a typical arrangement. Note the bridging rope that helps hold the trot together

If you are dealing with a Trot formed by timber piles then look for steel bars running up and down the piles with large steel rings on them. Your mooring lines will eventually be rigged as slip lines running through the rings, but there's no harm in using the bars temporarily while you get things sorted out. Buoys have large steel rings on top for the same purpose. It's common for boats to raft up two or three abreast between a single pair of piles, so if you are first in, be sure to moor securely.

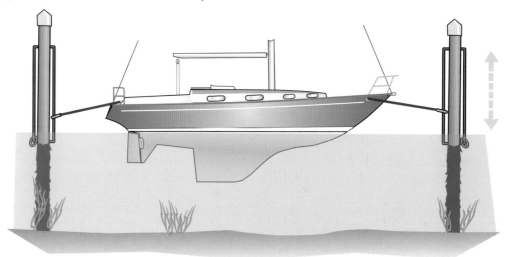

Fig 7:6 A trot with piles. The mooring ropes attach to sliding rings

APPROACH FOR TWIN ENGINE AND STEERABLE DRIVE BOATS

In the sequence shown in Fig 7:7, the wind is aligned at about 45° to the stream. The first boat into our Trot mooring is a twin screw diesel yacht. The skipper has sent crew forward to prepare the longest warp as a bow line with one end secured to the boat and the free end led outboard over the bow roller. He has also made ready a stern line and asked another crew to stand by with a 'wandering fender' in case he gets a little too close to the piles.

He then starts his run so as to approach the upstream pile bow first. He has chosen the line that's into the stream and almost into the wind. When he has brought his boat's bow close enough to the pile, the foredeck crew slips the bow line around the steel bar and then holds onto the end as the boat backs away from the pile. Using excellent reverse steering, the skipper now backs the boat towards the downstream pile as the foredeck crew eases out the bow line. If it all goes wrong and he runs out of line the crew can simply let go of his end and pull the line back on board without compromising the skipper's ability to manoeuvre. When the downstream pile is within reach, the crew stationed aft slips the stern line around the bar on the pile and, leaving a reasonable amount of slack, makes it fast. The foredeck crew can now haul in on the bow line to centre the boat between the piles. A steerable drive boat can use the same technique because they too have the ability to steer their sterns towards the downstream pile.

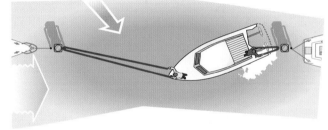

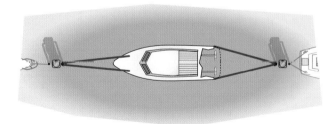

Fig 7:7

The crew of our twin engine boat have not quite finished. The half turns that they have in their mooring warps will wear through in no time if the bar is rough or rusty as the warp is pulled up and down it by water movement. So they should shuffle their boat forwards, find the sliding ring on the upstream bar and rig a new bow line through it, this time using a full turn (passing the line through the ring twice). After repeating the exercise with the stern line they can consider themselves safely moored.

APPROACH FOR SINGLE SCREW BOATS

If the skipper of a single screw boat had adopted the previous method he would almost certainly find that he was unable to steer the boat effectively in reverse. Without the wind he could possibly use the stream to control his stern as he dropped back, but the outcome would be uncertain. For him the answer is to slip the stern line first, then motor ahead forward to deal with the bow line. The stern line will need to be long, however, so that it can be paid out freely and not compromise any ability to steer forwards. One crew can be detailed as a 'wandering fender' and a second detailed to hold the end of the stern line at the mid-ships, widest, part of the boat.

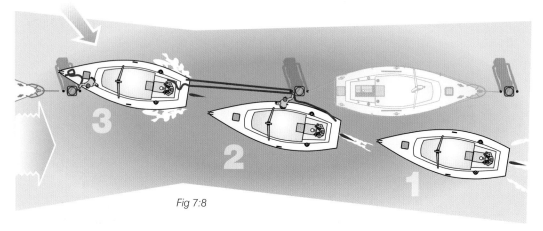

Fig 7:8

1 & 2: **Approaching so as to steer into the tide and be on the downwind side of the first pile our helm drives the boat gently up to position 2, close enough for the crew to pass the end of the stern line around the bar on the pile, take it aft and secure it to the boat's quarter.**

3: **As soon as the stern line has been successfully passed around the bar, the skipper then drives the boat forward placing the bow on the upwind side of the upstream pile so that the crew can pass a bow line around that bar and secure it. Once the bow line is secured a touch of reverse will be enough to start the boat drifting back away from the pile while the stern line is gathered in and the boat can be centred between the two piles.**

Once the boat has settled, the crew still have to go through the process of securing 'permanent' bow and stern lines with full turns through the sliding rings. Note that while one end of the stern line was the first to be secured the other end was left free to run until the bow line had been attached. If at any time the helm had to pull out of the manoeuvre, he could simply drive away pulling the stern line free of the pile and gathering it back on board.

STERN-TO MOORINGS

In many harbours where there's no significant stream, boats will moor 'stern-to' along a wall or jetty – an arrangement often known as a 'Mediterranean moor'. It's a simple way of getting more boats

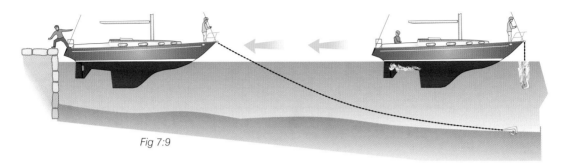

Fig 7:9

to the quay side without rafting up. But it's much more likely that you will be pushing into a gap between other boats, so use plenty of fenders on both quarters and beams, remembering to keep a large one for your stern.

As you approach, look for anchor chains over the bow rollers of the other boats already moored up. The presence (or otherwise) of chains will tell you what sort of mooring it is. Then find yourself a gap to squeeze into.

■ Start your reverse run from a long way off so that you establish good reverse control, then line yourself up with the mooring maybe four boat lengths out (Fig 7:9).

■ At about three boat lengths have your crew lower the anchor quickly and feel for it hitting the bottom. Continue to reverse as slowly as you dare while your crew pays out the anchor warp quite freely.

■ A couple of metres (6.6 feet) from the wall have your foredeck crew take the strain on the anchor warp and, as you reach stepping off distance, have another crew step ashore with two stern lines, one for each quarter. Once the shore crew has dropped their pre-prepared loops over the bollards, you can pull up on the anchor warp and adjust the stern lines so that the boat is held a half metre (19 inches) or so away from the quay (Fig 7:10).

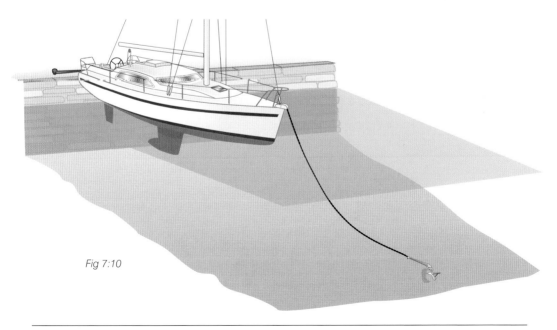

Fig 7:10

7

||||||||| MOORINGS ||||||||||||||||||||||||||||||||||||||||||||||||||||||||||||||||||||||||||||||||||||||||||||||||||||||||||||||||||||

Some people will prefer to do the whole thing the other way round, dropping their anchor over the stern and approaching the wall bows to – indeed, some flotilla charter companies prefer this approach. Some argue that they enjoy more privacy bows-to, but they need to make good provision for clambering ashore over the pulpit.

Lazy lines

Thankfully, since it's a more convenient arrangement by far, many harbour authorities provide lazy lines for their stern-to (or bow-to) moorings. These remove the need to drop your anchor. If you see ropes rather than anchor chains running from the other boats, you will know what to expect. Lazy lines normally – but by no means always – come in pairs. They lie on the seabed when not in use and are attached to the quay at one end and sinkers at the other.

The procedure is much the same as for a traditional stern to mooring but – of course, and very importantly – you don't drop your anchor. After securing your stern (or bow) lines, find the lazy lines and pull them up one on each side of your boat (or one side if there's only one line). Walk the lines to whichever end of the boat is to seaward, then tension them enough to draw the boat away from the wall, finally secure them to your cleats.

Again, this is a manoeuvre that can be done bows-to – and it is often much easier that way round.

Although a generally more satisfactory arrangement than anchoring, your security is dependent on the condition of the lazy lines. Check them for visible wear – particularly toward the end of the season.

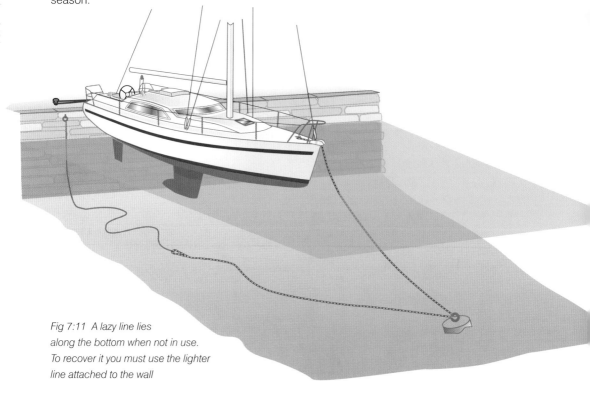

Fig 7:11 A lazy line lies along the bottom when not in use. To recover it you must use the lighter line attached to the wall

RAFTING

Rafting is common in crowded harbours, and calls for co-operation and consideration from all concerned

On busy quaysides and on some visitors' buoys, rafting up is the norm, and works well as long as everybody follows a few simple rules:

- Motor into the stream when coming alongside.

- Put out shore lines no matter how far you are from the quay, using loops on the bollards. If you don't rig shore lines then boats inside you cannot leave without casting you adrift. It's also both unfair and unwise to rely on other boats' mooring system and fittings.

- Adjust the lengths of the springs to keep your mast out of line with your neighbours' so that they cannot clash when the boats roll. You might also consider keeping the springs tight to avoid surging but leave the bow and stern lines relatively slack so that they don't snatch when the boats roll apart.

- Keep your fenders high and concentrated in the middle of the boat.

- To achieve all of this, you will almost certainly have to cross other boats. Do so quietly and via the foredeck. Except in the direst emergencies, never enter another's cockpit without permission.

- The same general rules apply when rafted up to a buoy. Make sure you run your own bow line to the buoy so other boats can leave whenever they want to.

So lets look at Fig 7:12 and see just how many mooring lines we need. The inside boat, first to arrive and alongside the quay has a bow line, a bow spring, a stern line and a stern spring all long enough to accommodate the rise and fall of the tide. The second and subsequent boats in should have put bow lines, springs, and stern lines to the adjacent boats and then shore lines from the bow and stern. Their shore lines have to be long enough to accommodate the range of the tide. The second boat in has made an approach in reverse to make sure that the rigs are well out of line and also to afford all three crews some privacy in their cockpits.

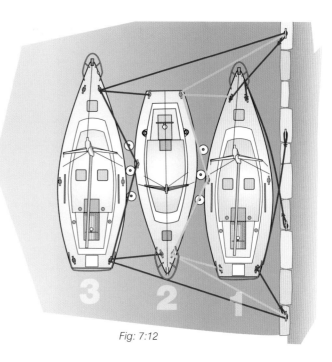

Fig: 7:12

LEAVING A RAFT

This is a relatively easy procedure – easy, that is, as long as you have a bit of co-operation from the boat outside you. Fig 7:13 shows a four-boat raft where the third boat out wants to leave. Having agreed to help, the crew of boat 4 have removed their stern shore line and re-rigged it around the stern of boat 3 attaching it to the bow of boat 2. Next they removed all of their lines from boat 3 except for their stern line. Boat 3 removed all of their lines from boat 2 except for their bow line. With the engine running and crew standing by, boat 3 is now ready to go. As boat 4 slips his stern line, boat 3 slips his bow line. The stream opens the gap between boats 4 and 2 and boat 3 motors forward clear of the raft. As she goes boat 4's crew haul in their new, long stern line and their bow shore line until they are snug alongside boat 2. They then have to re-rig bow line, springs and a stern shore line before they can relax.

Rafting is not necessarily relaxing, but great for social interaction and if you don't like the hustle and bustle of life on a town quay then you should pay your money and book a berth in a marina.

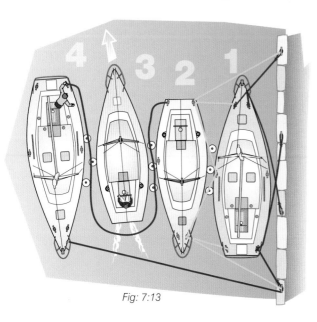

Fig: 7:13

8 HANDLING UNDER SAIL

In these days of crowded harbours and marinas, mooring under sail is pretty rare and, unsurprisingly, is usually discouraged by harbour masters. But the skill is really vital since engine failure is common and you need to be prepared for such an eventuality. All cruiser sailors should be able to use their sails to get themselves home. After all, dinghy and small keelboat sailors do it all the time. So, this section is not about sailing efficiently or squeezing the last ounce of speed from our sails, but about sailing a boat to a standstill under full control.

An obvious truth is that if we want to be able to slow down and stop, we have to be in a position to de-power the sails or spill wind. With most rigs it's not possible to spill wind from the mainsail if the wind is coming from more than an 80° angle from the bow (Fig 8:2) which means we can't use a mainsail if we want to make an approach with the wind coming from on or behind the beam. But if, say, we want to beat up to a berth or buoy, close hauled or close reaching, then the mainsail gives us the best slow speed control. Doing without a jib or genoa has the added benefit of keeping the foredeck clear for the crew handling the bow lines.

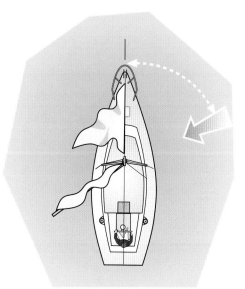

Fig 8:1 At about 60° to the wind both sails can be powered and de-powered at will ...

Having made your decision, reduce your sail area early, maintaining an efficient sailplan right up until the final approach. This might involve making a few rolls in the genoa and reefing the mainsail, but be warned: most modern sailing cruisers have relatively small mainsails and their jibs/genoas contribute a good part of the overall forward drive. So, while you may have been sailing along happily with a small jib and a couple of reefs in the main, you could suddenly find yourself underpowered when you drop the jib.

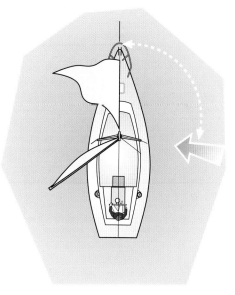

Fig 8:2 ... but with the wind on or abaft the beam the mainsail can not be eased

Flow around a fixed object is a good indicator of the strength and direction of the stream

SELECTING THE BEST LINE OF APPROACH

In tidal waters and rivers the decision on which line of approach to take depends, as ever, on the direction of the stream. Just because we are under sail makes no difference to our golden rule – we must still steer into, or as nearly as possible into, the stream.

Let's look at choices of approach line, to be made around a couple of mooring buoys. The same principles apply to pontoon or quayside berths.

Downwind and upstream
Figure 8:3 shows the ideal situation. Steering at the buoy, directly into the stream we have the wind from behind and, therefore, will use the jib alone on this approach. To slow the boat down as we get closer we can gradually roll the jib away or progressively drop it if it's a hanked sail. If we find that the boat is still moving too fast without any sail then we can execute a couple of big zig-zags. Turning the boat increases the surface area presented to the stream and takes the way off the boat. To judge speed, remember to use visual references on the beam rather than those ahead because it's speed over the ground that counts here, not speed through the water.

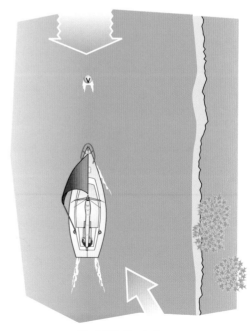

Fig 8:3 Sailing to buoy

Upwind and upstream

If wind and stream are directly aligned, you can approach the buoy close hauled on either starboard or port tack. But if they are slightly misaligned – as in Fig 8:4 – you should choose the tack that most closely heads the stream. However, to sail close hauled on starboard tack along the 'lay line' won't allow you to stop over the buoy. The problem is 'leeway' – the loss of ground to leeward suffered by all sailboats sailing close hauled. This effect will increase as you slow the boat down, so the best line of approach is that shown in Fig 8:5 (page 66).

There's a magical angle to the wind – about 60° – where you can both spill wind from your sails and power up again. By adopting this angle to the wind on our approach we can both slow down or speed up – in other words, have full control.

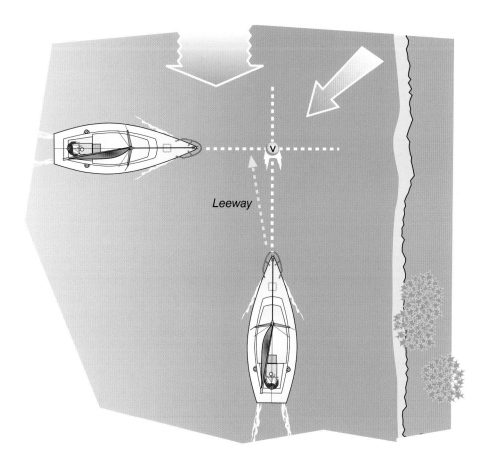

Fig 8:4 Sailing to buoy upwind

Looking at Fig 8:5, you can see that our helm chose a line some 20° above the lay line, pointing his bow a little upwind of the target buoy to allow for the inevitable leeway while still retaining an angle of about 60° to the wind. The skipper has decided to use the mainsail for good slow speed control.

1: **Here the crew starts to spill wind, allowing the boat to slow down. (The helm has noted a transit through the buoy to a moored yacht beyond.)**

2: **Now the mainsail trimmer realises that the boat is falling back on its transit so powers up the mainsail to speed up a little.**

3: **Having slightly overdone it and now advanced on the transit, he spills wind again to slow down and fall back.**

4: **Spot on. The helm turns into the stream and wind and the mainsail is fully eased to take the last little bit of way off the boat.**

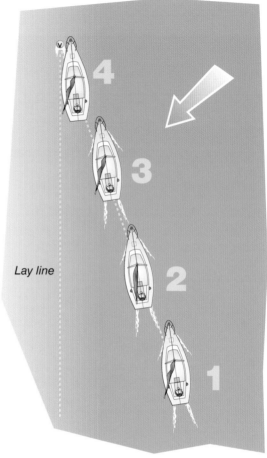

Lay line

Fig 8:5

A perfect approach. Yes, it's easier said than done, but you get the general idea. Don't be tempted to use steering to keep you on the transit. You went to a lot of trouble to get the angles right so why change them? Use acceleration and deceleration to keep you on line. Slowing down is not a huge problem with upwind approaches but if you are still going a knot too fast at the pick up point then 'back' the mainsail – that's to say push the boom out to leeward filling the sail on the wrong side.

Fig 8:6

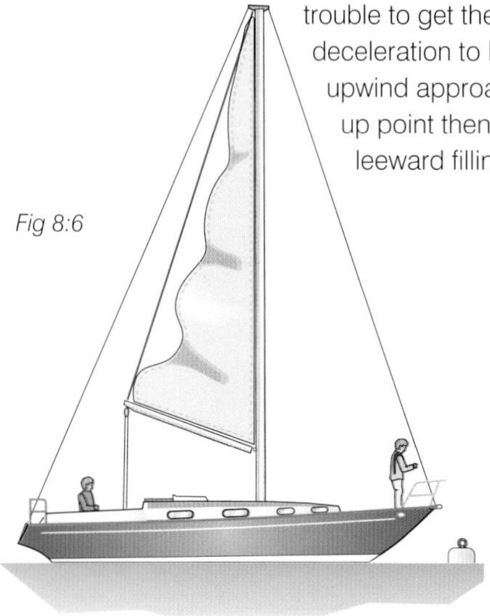

Scandalising

Having picked up the buoy, you will want to make sure that the mainsail doesn't start driving again. It's inconvenient to leave the boom swinging around at head level. The answer is to 'scandalise' the main. Ease the main sheet and vang, then lift the boom substantially on the topping lift. The boom can then be held in the middle of the boat by its sheet but the sail's shape will be completely spoiled and its ability to drive the boat will have been neutralised (Fig 8:6).

SAILING ONTO QUAYS OR PONTOONS

This is a manoeuvre that always seems daunting – no doubt because the point of contact is more solid. But the rules are really the same as for picking up buoys, starting with – you've guessed it! – heading into the stream.

Onshore wind ahead

In the first situation (Fig 8:7) we have a wind blowing onto a wall but when we approach head to stream then the wind will be coming over our port bow. As the wind is from ahead of the beam we will use our mainsail.

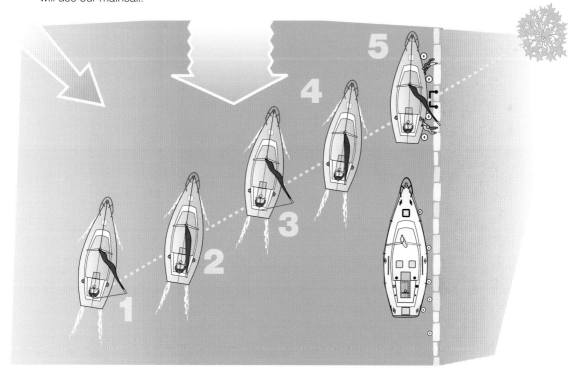

Fig 8:7

1: **Our helm has decided that there's enough stream to ferry glide and has picked a transit keeping a quayside tree a little to the right of his selected berth. He is spilling wind to slow down.**

2: **As he gets closer he notes that he is slipping downstream, so he powers up by pulling in on the mainsheet.**

3: **This brings him back onto his transit where he spills wind so as not to climb further.**

4 & 5: **Once more he slips back so powers up again to move back up onto transit ready to spill all the wind and touch down gently alongside.**

Wind abaft the beam

The second situation (Fig 8:8) sees the wind coming from over the starboard quarter, blowing just offshore, but this approach would be the same if wind were just onshore, coming from over the stern. In both cases, the jib is the appropriate sail to use. This time, our helm will progressively make the sail smaller in order to stay on the selected transit.

1: **Our helm has rolled away most of his jib in order to slow down and allow the stream to help him in.**

2: **Here he has slipped a little downstream and deployed a little more jib to move back up.**

3: **Coming alongside, he has rolled the jib away completely and secured temporarily to the ladder.**

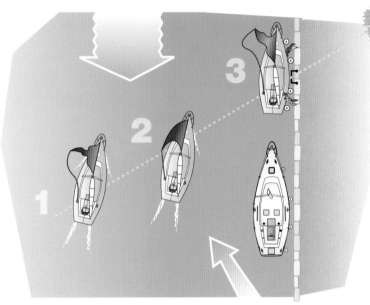

Fig 8:8

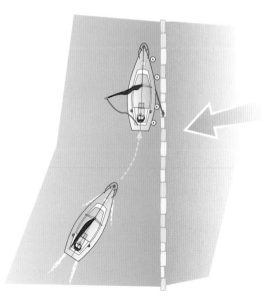

Offshore wind just forward of the beam

The yacht in Fig 8:9 has sailed close hauled towards the pontoon under mainsail. Knowing that he will be blown off the pontoon as soon as he stalls the boat, he makes a temporary connection with a short mid-ships spring and expects to have to use the spring to haul the boat back alongside.

Fig 8:9 Offshore wind just forward of the beam

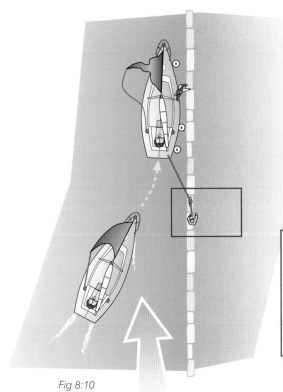

Fig 8:10

Surging

When coming alongside a wall downwind, it's very difficult to lose the last bit of boat speed. The skipper in Fig 8:10 has landed his crew with the stern line first with an instruction to take a turn on a wall cleat but to allow the line to slip a little as the strain comes on to avoid a shock loading to either cleat or rope (Fig 8:11). This is called 'surging' the boat to a halt and is kinder to all concerned than a violent stop.

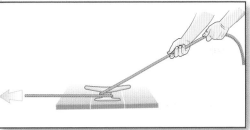

Fig 8:11

Sailing off

An offshore wind allows a boat to sail off the wall (Fig 8:12).

1: **The stern line is eased so the boat dangles downwind on its bow line. Now being head to wind, the sails are hoisted.**

2: **Next, the bow line is slipped. As the stern line becomes taut the sails are sheeted on, whereupon the stern line is slipped and the boat sails away.**

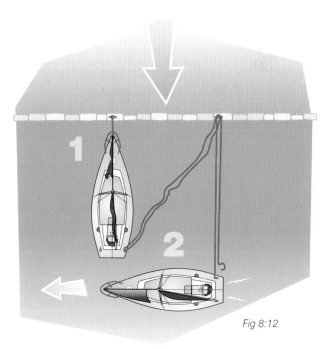

Fig 8:12

HEAVING TO

When at sea, it's really handy to be able to stop
your boat under sail. There are many occasions,
particularly if you sail short-handed, when you
just want to take the pressure off for a short
while: perhaps to wait for a tide to turn, set up
your mooring warps or simply put the kettle
on and have a bit of a break. The best way
of achieving this is to 'heave to'. Here's
how (Fig 8:13).

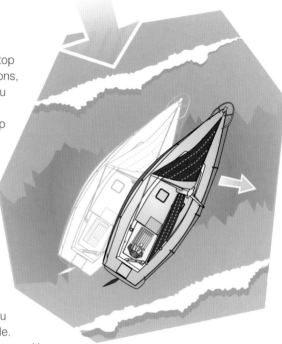

Fig 8:13 Hove to

■ First turn the boat through the wind
   (Fig 8:14). If you pull the main sheet
   in tight but leave the jib sheet just
   where it is, the wind will back the jib
   and increase the rate of turn until the
   mainsail starts to fill. As the mainsail fills,
   the turning action should stop, though you
   may need to help by steering to port a little.
   The boat should then be in a state of balance with
   the 'backed'
   jib pushing
   against the filled mainsail. The boat won't actually be
   stationary in terms of movement over the ground, but
   you won't be going anywhere very fast and you can
   certainly leave the helm to its own devices while you
   take care of the task in hand.

■ To sail away again simply release the windward
jib sheet and haul in on the other one. Obviously,
you will now have to tack if you want to resume your
original course.

Practise makes perfect

There are some points to consider before heaving
to. First make sure that you have enough sea room
and that you are not going to impede the progress
of other traffic. If you have a large genoa overlapping
the mast you may not want it backed against your
spreaders, so it may be a good idea to roll some
away before starting the manoeuvre. Finally, if you
don't want to tack into the hove to position then you
can always back the jib by hauling it up to windward
on the lazy sheet.

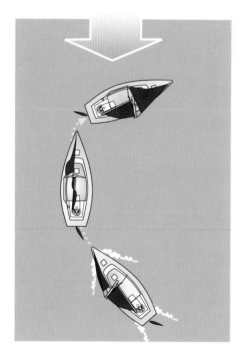

Fig 8:14

DOWNWIND SAILING

Bowling down the trade winds with the wind from over your quarter, at high boat speed and the expectation of a rum punch on a tropical island is the stuff of many sailors' dreams. Downwind sailing should be a pleasure in all climes, yet many sailors turn it into a rolling or gybing nightmare for the sake of a couple of extra lines and safety devices. So let's look at a couple of methods for making sure that your sleigh rides remain pleasures.

Preventers

If you want to run with a mainsail up for any length of time, rig a preventer. It will not stop you from gybing accidentally – that's down to the skill of the helm – but it will prevent the damage to gear and crew caused by the boom and mainsheet flying violently across the cockpit. They are very simple to rig. Take a line from the end of the boom, pass it around a strong point well forward on the boat and then return it into the cockpit where it can be tightened and made fast. In Fig 8:15 the red preventer line has been clipped to the boom end and then turned around the forward deck cleat before returning to a halyard winch via a turning block. As always there's more than one way to rig a preventer but I like the system shown for two reasons. Returning the line to the cockpit means that we can release it quickly if we need to gybe or to close up on the wind. Attaching it to the boom end ensures that the boom is supported if the end dips in the water on a heavy roll. Lines attached part way down the boom will produce an eccentric load and maybe a broken boom if the end were to catch a wave as the boat rolled.

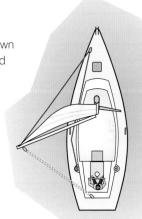

Fig 8:15

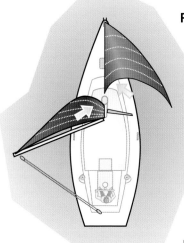

Fig 8:16

Rolling

Rolling from side to side, particularly coupled with a moderate or rough sea state, is very uncomfortable and tiring. Most of the rolling, however, is caused by excessive twist in sails. So it follows that if the sail twist is reduced then rolling can be controlled. Of course, we may have encouraged that twist deliberately. For instance, in light breezes we will often ease the mainsail vang and bring our genoa sheet leads aft to open our leeches, thereby allowing the tops of our sails to twist and produce more forward drive. The problem is that as the breeze builds the flow of wind over the upper part of the sails is deflected sideways inducing the rolling motion in the boat. Therefore, as the breeze increases we should remember to straighten our leeches by hardening down the mainsail vang and moving our genoa sheet leads forward.

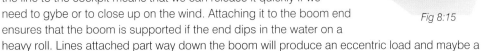

RYA Boat Handling for Sail and Power

Poling out headsails

When running or on a very deep broad reach, jibs and genoas are bound to set poorly in the mainsail's wind shadow. However, if we spread the headsail to windward – a technique knows as 'goose winging' or 'wing and wing' – it will be out of that wind shadow and will set effectively. Goose winging using the headsail sheet alone will only work for a few degrees above a dead run – and even then the sail will set and collapse repeatedly – but if the sail is sheeted through the end of a spinnaker pole the arrangement will work well for winds from dead aft to about 40° off the run. It's best to use a back guy (not shown here) on the pole to stop it swinging forward when the sheet is released.

The result will be a worthwhile improvement in boat speed as well as a nice balanced feel to the helm. What's more, with a couple of extra control lines we need not compromise our ability to tack or gybe the boat quickly.

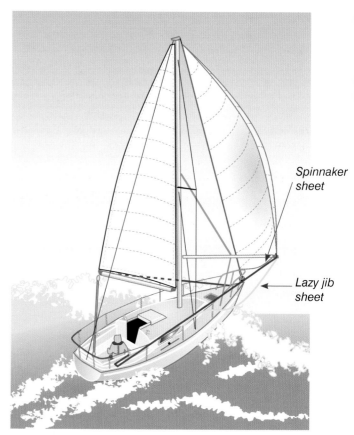

Spinnaker sheet

Lazy jib sheet

Fig 8:17 Use a spinnaker sheet through the pole end, leaving the jib sheets instantly usable

Mainsail or no mainsail?

Downwind sailing is tough on mainsails. When eased enough to run safely, they will often chafe on spreaders and rigging. More significant is their effect on the boat. With a large amount of sail area set well outboard, they have a tendency to turn the boat towards the wind – enough to cause broaching if the wind and sea state builds. In many circumstances it makes sense to drop the main and let the wind get to your genoa.

Twin headsails

To increase sail area when running or broad reaching under genoa you can set an additional jib 'poled out' to windward. The second jib can be set up loose luffed but be sure to fit a second lazy sheet and a back stay to the pole to make sail recovery easy. Some boats are set up for 'tradewind' sailing with twin forestays set close together and in line fore and aft. Both forestays can have roller genoas fitted or hanked on sails, but in any case coupled with two spinnaker poles produce a powerful but easily controlled downwind sail plan. Using any of these sail plans remember to keep the sail leeches pulled down straight to avoid rolling.

MOTOR SAILING

When the wind disappears, most of us will motor along with a mainsail hoisted waiting for the breeze to fill back in. In light breezes, using a little bit of engine to improve progress will increase boat speed and will push the 'apparent wind' forward so you become effectively close hauled. This means you will almost certainly need to sheet on to keep the sails drawing. If your intended course is too close to the apparent wind don't motor with flapping sails – they will act as brakes. As long as you have sea room, bear away enough for the sails to fill, and then tack towards your destination. Progress will be better.

Some sailing boats – particularly those built for comfort rather than speed – will not point high enough when the breeze builds. The losses to leeway become excessive. Such boats will benefit greatly from motor sailing, with a little bit of iron topsail improving their tacking angles tremendously. But, be warned: although the apparent wind won't move very far forward, the pressure on the sails will increase so you may have to think about reducing the size of headsails, in particular, as you increase the revs.

Cone

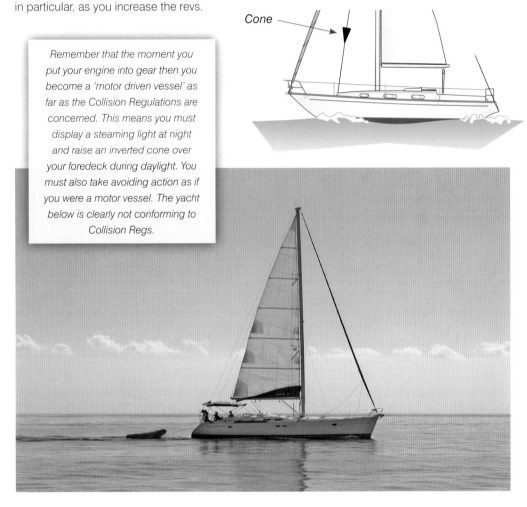

Remember that the moment you put your engine into gear then you become a 'motor driven vessel' as far as the Collision Regulations are concerned. This means you must display a steaming light at night and raise an inverted cone over your foredeck during daylight. You must also take avoiding action as if you were a motor vessel. The yacht below is clearly not conforming to Collision Regs.

9 ANCHORING

CHOOSING AN ANCHORAGE

It's easiest to start with deciding where not to anchor. Let's look at a few places to avoid and how they would be shown on charts.

 ■ This symbol means 'Anchoring Prohibited' and needs no further explanation.

 ■ Here we have 'foul ground' – a term that describes an area with the seabed contaminated by debris that may snag your anchor.

 ■ Wreck – again presenting a risk of snagging

ᴧᴧᴧᴧ∫ᴧᴧᴧ ■ Next we have 'Underwater Cables'. You don't want to chance hooking your iron anchor around a 33,000V electricity cable so clearly these must be avoided.

For a full list of warning symbols you should consult the Admiralty List of Symbols and Abbreviations (available from the RYA Webshop, Code 5011). But, in addition to specific hazards, you should avoid tide races, seabeds where there's lots of rock or kelp – neither of which allow an anchor to take a grip – and bottoms that shelve too steeply. Lastly don't anchor in Marked Channels, where you might obstruct shipping.

So where should we anchor?

It's all common sense really. We are looking for a place that's sheltered from wind, stream and swell, that has a reasonably flat bottom and 'good holding' – that's to say a material you can imagine your anchor ploughing into and holding fast – mud, clay or sand being ideal. You should also choose a place where you will still be afloat when the tide goes out and where it won't be too deep when it comes in. Finally, you need to give yourself room to swing, clear of rocks, other boats and anywhere where there might be heavy traffic movements. Easy!

Many recommended anchorages are marked on charts as 'Small Craft Anchorage' or with an anchor symbol. Beware of the latter. They could be talking about aircraft carriers with accompanying battle fleets rather than your 35 foot family cruiser.

Let's say that you are motoring into a bay with a good holding bottom sheltered from wind and swell etc. There are plenty of other boats already there and you need to find a good place to anchor with about three metres (ten feet) depth at low water. You've checked for underwater hazards and there are none, but you need to consider what the other anchored vessels will do as the stream and wind change. If we assume that the other boats are anchored properly we can assume that they will have veered up to six times the maximum depth of water. We should consider where their anchors might be, so that we don't end up lying over one. Then think about where the other boats will lie after any change in wind and tide so they don't end up laying over our anchor. In the chart Fig 9:1, motor yacht **C** is laying to the wind while the deep keeled sailing yachts are lying to the stream. At first glance dropping the hook astern of **C** and laying back between **C** and

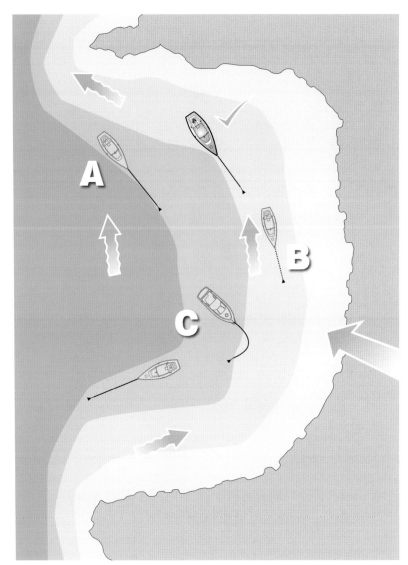

Fig 9:1 Choosing the best spot to anchor involves a number of important considerations

A looks quite attractive until you consider that **A** might swing over your anchor as the stream changes, additionally you would probably swing at a different time compared with the motor yacht with the potential for a clash of hulls. So you choose to anchor a couple of boat lengths astern and inshore of **B**. Finally you take bearings on the buildings ashore to make sure that you are firmly anchored and then work out when the tide turns making a mental note to be on deck at that time.

Anchoring out in unfamiliar waters is never comfortable but, to stay out of trouble, check the chart for hazards. Keep away from other boats, particularly those with different underwater profiles. Think about changes in wind and stream direction and watch out for boats anchoring too near to you.

ROPE OR CHAIN?

There's no doubt that an anchor warp (or 'rode') made up solely of chain is better than one comprising part chain and part nylon rope. The boat will sit easier and be safer with an all chain warp. A combination of chain and rope is an acceptable arrangement for smaller boats, but rope alone is only suitable for the very lightest duties.

Bruce

A good all-purpose anchor but awkward to stow

Danforth

Awkward stowed in a bow roller but lies flat in lockers. Liable to pinch your fingers. Works well in mud or sand but not good in rocks or weed

CQR

A popular perennial that has been around for decades. It performs well on a wide range of seabed types

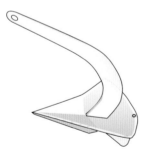

Spade

A relatively new self-stowing anchor that is gaining a good reputation for versatility and efficiency

Fisherman

Great in rock or weed but inefficient in pretty much everything else

Delta

A rigid version of the CQR and reputed to be as efficient

COMING TO ANCHOR

Let's say that you are coming to anchor under engine in a busy anchorage. You have selected a nice gap, free of danger and where you are unlikely to drop your hook over someone else's warp.

■ Take a look at the way other boats like yours are lying and approach your spot from a similar angle.

■ Stop the boat over your chosen position and lower the anchor quickly until your crew feels it touch the bottom.

■ On their signal you should reverse slowly while they continue to pay out the anchor warp to the required length. Lay the warp out in as straight a line as possible.

■ Finally, 'set' the anchor with a strong tug in reverse to dig it well in (Fig 9:2).

If your anchor warp is all chain then you should make the anchor warp at least four times the maximum depth of water that you will experience over the tidal range. That should be enough to hold you tight. If using a mixture of rope and chain then increase that ratio to at least six times the depth.

When you think that you are secure, take a transit or a bearing on a fixed object on your beam. If it remains constant then you can be sure you are not dragging, that is slipping over the seabed. If there are no transits or fixed objects in view, lean over the bow and hold the anchor warp. If you're dragging you will feel the vibration as the anchor slides over the ground.

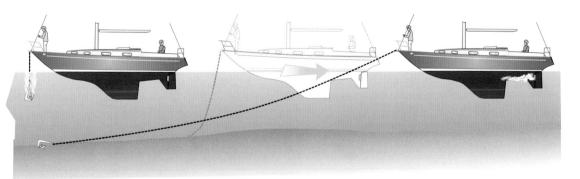

Fig 9:2

TIP Mark your chain every five metres with painted links, pieces of coloured line or plastic cable ties in some recognisable manner. Then record the marking system so that you remember it and can explain it to others.

9

SAILING TO ANCHOR

The techniques for anchoring under sail are much the same as under power – except that you don't have reverse power. To overcome this you may need to back your sails to encourage the boat to reverse away (Fig 9:3). This is not a problem if the wind and stream are from roughly the same direction, but if they are contrary and you are using a rope and chain warp, you must be careful that the stream doesn't twist the boat around the warp, wrapping it around your keel. If the worst does happen, you may consider buoying the bitter end of your warp and dropping the whole thing overboard. As the warp slackens it should sink away from the boat so that you can bring the boat back to the buoyed end for a recovery.

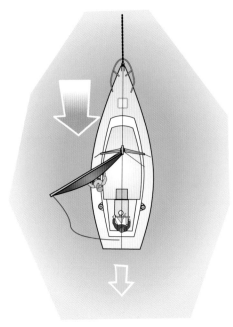

RAISING THE ANCHOR

Fig 9:3

Recovering the anchor is easiest if you have a powerful, motor driven windlass. In which case you can simply winch the anchor back on board and then drive away.

Just remember that your boat will move towards the anchor, not the other way round. If your crew are hauling the anchor by hand then you can make life a lot easier by motoring very gently towards it. Once the warp is 'straight up and down' wait in neutral while the crew break it out of the seabed and haul it up to the bow, before driving away.

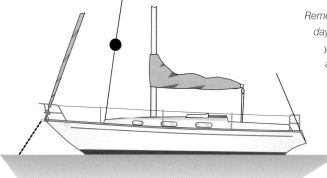

Remember: always display an anchor ball during daylight or an anchor light at night to show that you are anchored. Anchor warps and chains are difficult to see when approaching a boat from ahead. Under those circumstances an anchored boat with a stream bubbling around the bow could look just like a boat motoring gently ahead with potentially disastrous consequences in terms of avoiding collision.

TIP On some boats, the chain piles up on the base of the locker until it jams. To prevent this happening, you may want to have a crew below to arrange it neatly.

10 TOWING

TOWING FROM THE STERN

When towing in open water, the essential points to remember are:

- Use as long a towline as possible, preferably of a stretchy rope – nylon being ideal.

- Try to adjust the length of the towline so the tug and tow are on similar parts of the wave cycle. That way you won't find the tow surfing towards your stern while you are struggling up a wave face.

- Considerable shock loads can occur when towing and 'normal' deck fittings may not be up to the task. So, both tug and tow can benefit from rigging a second strong rope as a yoke over stern or bow and then secure the yoke to as many strong deck fittings as you can sensibly include. On sailing boats, the sheet winches often provide useful attachment points. To attach the towline to the yoke, use a knot that can be undone under load, the round turn and two half hitches being a good choice.

- Abrasion can be severe, both to the ropes and to your boat, so do what you can to guard against it by wrapping any rubbing points with cloths.

- If conditions are rough, consider hanging a weight from the mid point of the towline to help reduce shock loads.

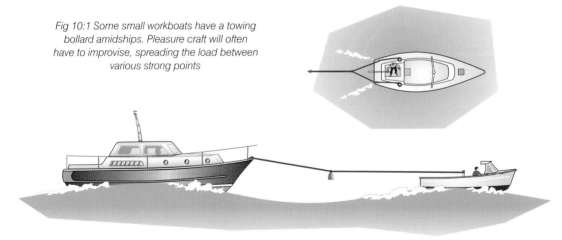

Fig 10:1 Some small workboats have a towing bollard amidships. Pleasure craft will often have to improvise, spreading the load between various strong points

Towing astern seriously compromises the steering ability of the towing vessel. The effective pivot point moves back behind the attachment point for the tow line so helmsmen need to be conscious of the need to steer through large circles. It really helps if the towed vessel is steered to follow the tug. Crew should keep a watch on the tow and the deck fittings securing the tow line.

ALONGSIDE TOWS

Once you have dragged your tow into sheltered waters you can shorten the towline and strap it alongside. Alongside tows are used to improve the handling characteristics of the whole arrangement to the point where you can even place the tow in a berth.

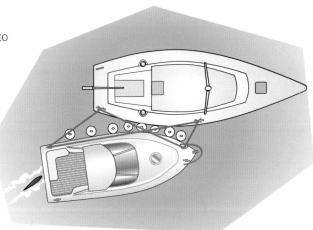

Fig 10:2 *Because of the drag to port, this tug will need some starboard helm to compensate*

You will want to use plenty of fenders between the two boats and will need a bow line, stern line, bow spring and stern spring to keep them firmly attached with the minimum of movement between them. If both tow and tug are sailing boats, do your best to keep the rigs out of line so that they don't clash if you are hit by a large wash. If the yachts are single engine, with fin or twin keels, it's best to arrange for the tow to be placed across the tug's bow, as shown above, so that the steering pivots of the boats are as close in line as possible.

Twin engined tugs will find it easier to steer when pushing than a single engine vessel, but neither should have much trouble, provided they take it steady and think through the manoeuvres and limitations carefully. For instance, if you have the tow on your port bow, it will be easier to turn to port than to starboard because of the inertia and drag of the tow. Then when you go into reverse to slow or stop, the tug will stop but the tow will keep going, causing the whole arrangement to rotate. It's helpful to find out in advance what awaits you at your destination, since the knowledge may determine which side of your boat you decide to place the tow.

Even in sheltered waters a wash from a passing motor boat can cause violent movements between the tug and tow. Crew should keep a close watch on the fenders, attaching warps and the deck fittings on both boats to give early warning of any failures. Again it can help if the tow is steered to match the tug.

The International Regulations for the Prevention of Collision at Sea (or Colregs as they are sometimes called) require both the tug and tow to carry a diamond shaped day mark during daylight hours and the lights shown at night. At night the tow carries running lights, red to port, green to starboard and white over the stern, because she is underway but not under power. The tug carries the same running lights showing that she is underway, a white steaming light to show that she is under power plus two more white steaming lights plus an extra yellow stern light to show that she is towing with a long tow.

In the case of a short tow (tow length less than 200m (656 feet)) the day marks are not required, I guess because it should be obvious, but at night the tow carries the same lights as above while the tug is almost the same. She carries one extra white steaming light instead of two. In the event of emergencies, neither may be practicable.

---

11 HEAVY WEATHER

The term 'heavy weather' means different things to different boaters. Smaller sailing and motor cruisers in open water would probably consider a Force 5 heavy, whereas a well found fifty footer could be happy with a Force 7. In fact using wind strength alone to define heavy weather can be misleading since it isn't really strong winds that are the problem. Of more importance is the sea state that is stirred up by the general conditions, and the wind is only one of the factors involved. The others are the strength and direction of the stream and the topography of both the seabed and any nearby land.

Long ocean swells that swoop up and down are usually benign. The real mischief is done by the short, steep waves with deep 'holes' between them. These are produced by local conditions. A lot of heavy weather damage occurs when falling into the troughs between the waves.

The severest sea state is often to be found where the water is shallow – for instance, over sand bars and rocky ledges where the rolling mass of water is pushed upwards until it breaks (Fig 11:1). Also where the wind direction is in opposition to the tidal stream and around headlands, and where charts are marked with 'overfalls'. Good seamen will take all of these conditions into account when planning their passages, and avoid them if they can.

Fig 11:1

WEATHER FORECASTS

With modern communications, weather forecasts are easy to obtain, and usually very accurate in predicting wind strength and direction. However, we should understand their shortcomings, particularly with regard to the sea state. Look at the problem that the meteorologist faces when asked to forecast the size of waves. He starts with a perfectly sound scientific appraisal of what the wind is doing but is then asked to come up with a one-word description of the sea state for a long stretch of coast and up to 12 nautical miles offshore. That sea area will include sheltered bays, exposed headlands with shallow ledges and – worse still – tidal streams of variable velocity that will change direction through 180° within the forecast period. He can't possibly describe the conditions in every location so takes a general view of the sea state in open water created by the wind alone.

Let's say that the forecaster gives us a Force 5 wind and a moderate sea state. We must look at that prediction of wave height objectively and realise that, while we might find calmer conditions in the lee of the land, we might encounter dangerously rough seas in the overfalls off the headland, when the stream runs against the wind. It's up to us to make these seamanlike judgements for ourselves, and then plan our passages to suit our prediction of the sea conditions and our boat's ability to handle them.

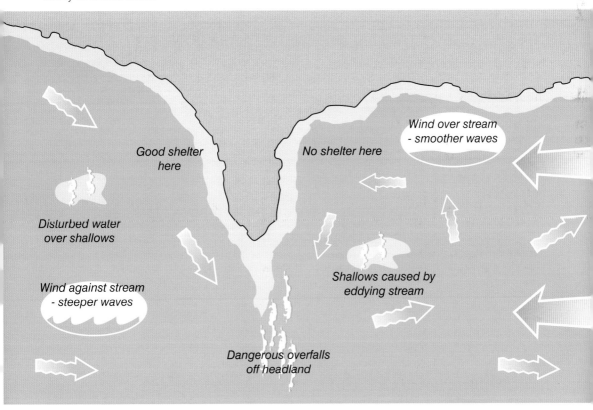

Fig 11:2 Conditions can vary greatly from place to place

BREAKING WAVES AND BROACHING

Breaking waves don't just occur in shallow water – they can be found far from land. And they are dangerous, possibly dumping large amounts of water onto (or into) your boat with a significant negative effect on both stability and directional control. If you are unlucky enough to be caught broadside on to a breaking wave having a height larger than your boat's beam, you can be rolled over by the dynamic forces within the wave – no matter how much stability your boat possesses.

Broaching is an uncontrollable turn across the wind. It can happen for three reasons:

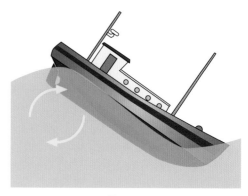

Fig 11:3

■ Any boat running down a heavy sea may surf into the back of the next wave ahead, burying the bow. When the boat stops the following wave will carry its stern around leaving the boat beam on to the seas. (Fig 11:3)

■ A boat's rudder or rudders may lift out of green water as a wave crest lifts its stern. With no helm control the boat can again be turned by the wave into that critical beam-on situation. (Fig 11:4)

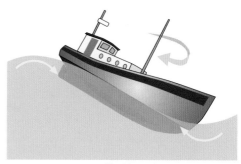

Fig 11:4

■ On a sailboat running with too much sail up, weather helm may increase to the point where the rudder stalls and the boat will turn across the wind and probably heel significantly to leeward. (Fig 11:5)

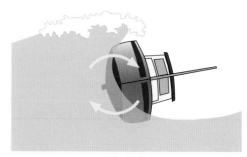

Fig 11:5

TIP To avoid broaching, sailing boats should take down all sail from behind the mast, and slow down by reducing headsail area. Power vessels should simply throttle back until they are going a little slower than the waves.

DROGUES

In extreme circumstances we can trail long warps or a drogue over the stern to both slow our boat down and move the natural pivot points back towards the stern. This leaves a boat with compromised steering but any tendency to broach is significantly reduced.

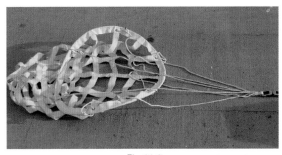

Fig 11:6

A purpose made drogue is essentially an open-ended canvas or webbing bucket on the end of a very long, heavy warp (Fig 11:6). It can be deployed from the stern of a boat on the centreline and dragged through the water in order to slow the vessel down and keep the stern pointing into the wind and heavy following seas.

A 'series drogue' is a length of warp with numerous canvas chutes attached along its length and is probably more effective. A drogue can be improvised from lengths of mooring warp tied together and deployed in a long loop from one quarter of the boat to the other.

The key to success with any drogue is length. The drogue needs to grip in the water at least one whole wave period behind the boat (Fig 11:7). Too short, and a big wave could bundle it all up and throw it back on board. Drogues do work but they also make steering difficult, just as if you are towing another vessel, so if using the system for real, make sure that you have plenty of sea room!

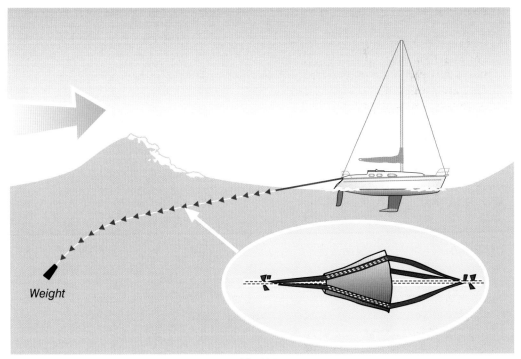

Weight

Fig 11:7

STORM AND HEAVY WEATHER SAILS

When some sailing yachts race offshore they must carry a trysail (see ISAF regulations), a heavy-weather jib (made of a non-exotic material, usually a stout polyester) and also a storm jib in addition to their usual sail wardrobe. Although not obligatory for cruisers, this is a sensible inventory for all offshore yachts.

Storm jib

This is really the only true 'storm sail' in the kit, since in survival conditions the only directional option is downwind, so you only need a tiny sail set towards the bow to give you steerageway. A storm jib, therefore, is not cut for speed but for ease of control. Most are set up on a tack strop so that the whole sail sets well above deck level, making it less likely to catch a wave and allowing the sheets to lead back to a regular car position. Most storm jibs are made a highly visible colour to make the boat easier to spot in stormy seas.

If the storm jib has a bolt rope intended to run up a luff groove, there should be an alternate arrangement for attaching it to the forestay in the event of luff damage.

If you have a furling genoa on a single forestay then you need an effective method for attaching your storm jib to the forestay with the genoa still in place – including a second halyard to hoist it.

Trysail

Trysails are heavy weather mainsails, set loose footed and low on the mast. They are great sails for close reaching, producing lots of forward drive with very little heel. They can't be trimmed to sail close hauled but, once the sea state has become so large that you have to bear away (to say 55° off the wind) to avoid falling into wave troughs, then trysails give you a much easier ride than heavily reefed mainsails.

Trysails are normally sheeted independent of the boom, down to blocks on the quarters – often the spinnaker sheet blocks. Serious offshore cruisers have independent mast tracks to set them on, so that they can be rigged before the mainsail is dropped. If the wind and sea state rise to the point where you are forced to run downwind, the trysail should be dropped. It won't set well on a run and in those circumstances any sail area behind the mast will encourage broaching.

Heavy weather jib

Many would say that every yacht should be equipped with a heavy weather jib (approximately a No. 4 size) that would balance nicely with either a fully reefed main or a trysail. It should be capable of being set fairly low in the rig on either the forestay or an inner forestay. The sail should be made from heavy polyester and provide good forward drive for close or beam reaching across a heavy sea. This applies particularly to those yachts that rely on a single large furling genoa – a sail typically far too light for heavy weather and setting hopelessly when deep reefed. They can blow fully open in strong winds, becoming very difficult, even dangerous to control. So think about rolling away those big genoas completely when the wind rises and set an independent heavy weather jib that can't get out of control.

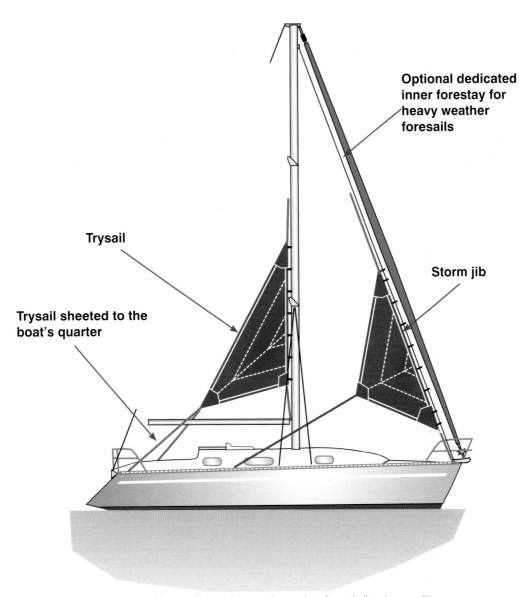

Optional dedicated inner forestay for heavy weather foresails

Trysail

Storm jib

Trysail sheeted to the boat's quarter

Fig 11:8 All offshore sailing yachts must be ready to face challenging conditions. Proper heavy weather sails will make life much more tolerable.

TIP It's no good just carrying storm and heavy weather sails. You must practise setting them in calm conditions so that all of the crew know how to run the sheets etc. Bouncing around the foredeck of a small yacht in a gale is not the time to work out how the storm jib sets.

DRIVING OVER WAVES

Taking any boat to windward in heavy conditions can be an uncomfortable experience – but much depends upon the skill of the helmsman. Let's see how a motor and a sailing boat might handle worsening conditions.

Motor yacht
- Our motor yacht sets out into a Force 3 with a slight to moderate sea state, enjoying a high speed ride towards its destination.

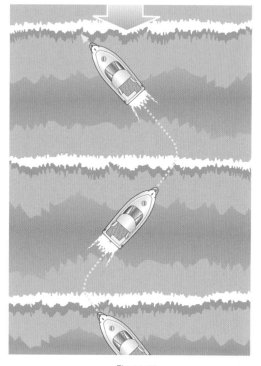

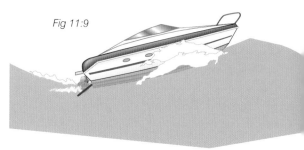

Fig 11:9

- The wind increases to a Force 4 and the waves become larger. The helm trims the bow down to reduce the tendency to launch off the wave tops. (Fig 11:9)

- As the wind rises another notch, the helmsman decides to slow down into displacement mode to stop the boat from crashing off the waves. He adopts a zig-zag course over the waves to lengthen the run between wave crests. (Fig 11:10)

Fig 11:10

- Finally with wind nearing gale force and the waves increasing in size the skipper decides to abandon his plan and run for shelter downwind. His challenge now is to avoid burying his bow in the back of the wave ahead so he trims the bow up and adjusts his speed to run a little slower than the waves while adopting a shallow zig-zag course towards shelter, taking care to avoid broaching. (Fig 11:11)

Fig 11:11

Sailing yacht

- Our sailing crew sets off in a mid-size cruiser towards their home port. At first they have a full mainsail and a working jib set for Force 3 but, with a forecast of stronger winds to come, they have donned waterproofs, lifejackets and harnesses and dug the trysail and storm jib out from the bottom of the locker.

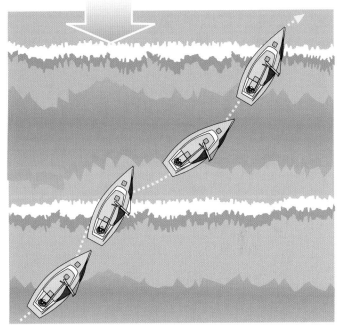

Fig 11:12

- The wind rises to Force 5, sooner than anticipated, and the skipper feels that they are going too fast close hauled so calls for 2 reefs in the mainsail and bears away a little to avoid launching off the waves.

- With the wind rising to Force 6/7 the helmsman finds that he has to bear away a little more to ride easily down the back of the waves and then head up a little to climb the next (Fig 11:12). The skipper decides that the trysail would be more appropriate than the reefed mainsail.

- Later still, the wind has risen to a full gale. The ride is now very uncomfortable and progress to windward is extremely slow, so the skipper decides that enough is enough and calls for a change of course back downwind to find a sheltered port. Bearing away onto a broad reach the crew drop the trysail and settle in for a sleigh ride under jib alone towards their haven.

Both of the above scenarios ended in conditions that the boats could handle. In more extreme, storm conditions they each may have had to slow their boats down by changing to a storm jib, throttling back, or trailing warps or a drogue. In those circumstances there is a real danger of being 'pooped' (taking a wave over the stern) so all cockpit hatches and vents should be closed and washboards put in place. All crew on deck must be harnessed to the boat, the most exposed with two tethers.

TIP Be prepared! When you call for crew to go forward to reduce sail, they should already be wearing sea boots, oilies and lifejackets. Also, harnesses should be clipped on in heavy weather.

12 EMERGENCIES

GROUNDINGS

They say that every sailor will run aground eventually
– and you should consider yourself lucky if you do it
only once. All it takes is to push on a little too far when
tacking up a shallow river or to try too hard to cheat
the tide by venturing into the shallows.

If you do go aground, the ideal boat to do it in is
a fin keeled yacht, since they have the best chance
of getting off quickly. By heeling a fin keeler, you can
reduce its draught, hopefully to the point where you
can reverse off a bank using the engine.

There are various ways of heeling the boat:

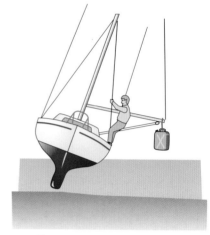

*Fig 12:1 Heeling a fin keeler will
reduce its draught....*

■ If the wind is in the right direction and you are on
the leeward side of the bank, sheeting in the sails
might do the trick.

■ All moveable weights – including the crew – can
be transferred to one side, even possibly hanging
something heavy, such as a jerrycan filled with
water, on the end of the boom and swinging it
outboard.

■ If none of the above works then a tow off may be
required. If heavily aground, a useful technique
is to attach the tow line to a spinnaker halyard
and tow very gently from the abeam. The boat
will heel, lifting the keel and dragging you off
sideways off the mud. The same effect can be
gained by rowing out an anchor abeam and
hardening down on the halyard winch.

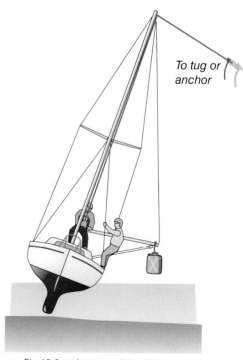

To tug or
anchor

Twin keeled sailboats are not so easy to release from
the mud. If they go on upright, heeling the boat will
only dig one keel in further. The best chance comes
from loading as much spare weight as possible into
the bow then motoring or towing out astern.

*Fig 12:2 ... but you might still need a
tow from the masthead to get you off*

Fig 12:3 Embarrassing but not usually dangerous on sand, mud or shingle in reasonable conditions

It's best not to put a motorboat aground, since there is a real possibility of damaging propellers, drive units or rudders. If you are aground then the best way off is directly astern putting spare weight into the bow to lift the back end, but it's a calculated risk! If you didn't damage the gear underneath the boat on the way on then you may do so on the way off and the silt and gravel stirred up from the bottom when you engage reverse will be pumped straight into your raw water intake. So it might be better to wait for a tow or a rising tide.

To tug or anchor

Fig 12:4 Heeling won't work with twin keelers. But getting some weight forward often will

WARNING: Sliding into soft mud in a river estuary will probably only damage a skipper's reputation but hitting rocks or gravel can cause structural damage to a boat. After any such incident check the keel mounting inside the hull immediately. Check for cracks in the hull before and behind the keel, around the keel bolts and the sub-structures that support the keel. In particular look for signs of water ingress. If in any doubt then have the underside inspected by a surveyor at the earliest opportunity.

RYA Boat Handling for Sail and Power

MAN OVERBOARD (MOB)

If anybody falls off of a vessel underway, you have a life-threatening situation – certainly one that demands a Distress (Mayday) call. In reasonable conditions it might seem that the chances of recovering the casualty are very good, but things have a tendency to go from bad to worse, in which case you will need the assistance of the rescue services. Even if you recover the MOB, he may have been injured, might be hypothermic or in shock – in which case a medical evacuation may be required. So make the distress call as soon as possible.

But, the question is when? If you have crew members to spare, there's no problem. Detail one of them to make the call while you go about organising the recovery. If short handed you will have to prioritise your actions. If you have a VHF radio with DSC facility, consider pressing the distress button on your DSC set early. This will then send an automatic distress message and give the Coastguard a position. You can get back to the voice message later. Or perhaps you could use a handheld VHF while remaining in the cockpit.

First reactions

When somebody goes over the side we need to get back to them as soon as possible, because in cold water their potential survival time may not be long. Of great importance are:

- The need to stay as close as possible throughout the manoeuvre, so that we don't lose sight of them.
- Avoiding injury to the MOB in our approach, either with the prop, by running him down, or by having the boat crash down on him in heavy seas. This means we must approach him carefully and at a controlled speed.
- Lastly, we must maintain our ability to manoeuvre.

LIFEJACKETS AND SAFETY HARNESSES

Accidents can happen but we can minimize the risks. Sailboat crew members, particularly in rough conditions and always at night, should tether themselves to the boat when on deck. Each tether should have an approved type safety hook (right) 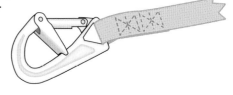 and should be rigged in such a manner as to make it almost impossible for the wearer to go overboard – that's to say the length of the tether and the position of its securing point should not allow you beyond the guardwires or rails.

Total protection is often impracticable. For example, sailing yachts often have jackstays rigged along their side decks. Clipped to the weather jackstay you have good security if thrown to leeward – by far the most likely risk – but remain vulnerable to falling overboard to windward.

Harnesses and lifejackets are often combined as shown opposite:

The problem is that a manoeuvre that works well on one boat could be disastrous on another. For instance, a slow moving displacement motorboat might immediately put its engine controls into neutral and carry out a quick turn, while a sudden stop on a fast moving, planing boat might well lead to injuries among those still aboard. And while a sailing cruiser with a fixed backstay can immediately turn through the wind (heave to) in order to stop close to the casualty, an old gaffer or racing yacht with running backstays might well lose their rig if they attempted the same. Before we look at what manoeuvres might work best for various boat types, it's worth noting that none of them involve approaching the casualty directly upwind.

In all cases, the first reaction should be:

■ The first person to see the emergency should shout 'MAN OVERBOARD' to alert the whole crew and if possible point at the casualty, and continue to do so in order not to lose sight.

■ Someone should press the MOB button on the GPS or chart plotter and the distress button on a DSC radio.

■ Keep visual contact and launch specific rescue gear off the back of the boat.

Immediately we start to talk about what to do first we come up against the problem of suggesting something that is inappropriate for a particular boat type. The truth is that you cannot drill for this eventuality because you don't know who is going to fall off – maybe the skipper! You definitely need to practise to find a good system for your boat and everybody on board needs to understand what must to be done to make your system work. Whoever is on the helm should be capable of starting the recovery procedure without injuring others. At the end of the day be prepared to be inventive. Don't sail off through a figure of eight if a quick burst of astern power will put you alongside the casualty. From the casualty's point of view the quickest successful method will be the best, no matter how inelegant.

Having said that here are some methods for various boat types that will work.

Whether tethered or not, lifejackets should always be worn when:

■ In an open boat such as a small power boat or when going ashore in a yacht tender.

■ By children on deck at all times.

■ At all times if you are a non-swimmer and there is any possibility of you entering the water.

■ On deck at night or in rough conditions.

■ Whenever the skipper deems it necessary.

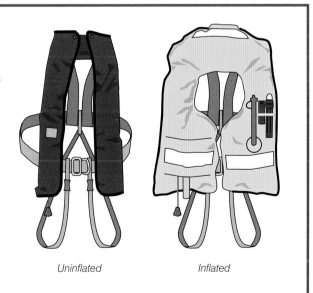

Uninflated   *Inflated*

RYA Boat Handling for Sail and Power

Sailing cruisers

Modern sailing cruisers have relatively small mainsails and efficient auxiliary engines. They should use their sails to stop the boat and then use their engines to manoeuvre for a pick up.

1: **The casualty falls off while the boat is cruising along nicely on a beam reach.**

2: **As soon as he is aware of the problem the helm turns the boat through the wind, effectively heaving to. The engine is started.**

3: **The mainsail is sheeted in tight to reduce any drive from it and to prevent it swinging across the cockpit. If the backed jib is in the way it can be rolled away or dropped.**

4: **The skipper then drives the boat to a stop upwind of the casualty and across the wind. Using reverse and forward drive as required he allows the boat to drift down onto the casualty beam on. The MOB is recovered from the leeward side.**

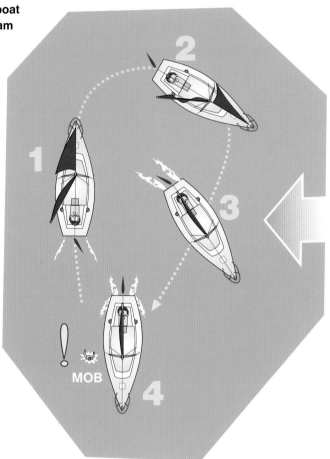

Fig 12:6 The agility of modern sailing yachts makes returning for the MOB relatively simple

There are several advantages to this approach. It's gentle, the boat and casualty rise and fall together with any wave action, the boat provides a lee to the MOB and the connection should be positive without any tendency for the boat to drift away. Furthermore, in strong winds the boat will be heeled towards the casualty making the pick up easier.

Sailing yachts with large mainsails, running backstays, etc.

Some yachts can not be 'crash tacked' without risking losing the rig and making an already dire situation worse. Any sailboat with a powerful mainsail – one that will out-power their engines – or running backstays essential for supporting its mast falls into this category. These boats need a little bit of crew organisation before they tack, and their final approach line should be at that magical 60° to the wind (see page 63) so their mainsails can be eased and left shaking (de-powered) through the final stages of the manoeuvre.

1: **The casualty goes overboard with the boat close hauled.**

2: **The skipper bears away onto a beam reach as soon as he is aware of the MOB. He tells the crew to prepare to tack the boat, dropping the jib in the tack.**

3: **Once through the wind, he bears away onto a broad reach and starts the engine.**

4: **Easing the mainsail completely, the skipper turns his leeward bow towards the casualty.**

With the mainsail flapping and de-powered, he can now use the engine to manoeuvre the boat to a standstill with the casualty alongside his leeward beam, ready for a pick up.

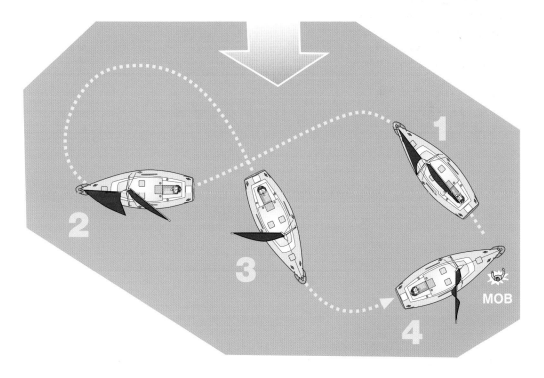

Fig 12:7 To avoid damage to their rigs, some yachts demand rather gentler handling

Large motor boats

1: At somewhere above 20 knots, a crew member falls off the stern.

2: Having heard the Man Overboard call, the helmsman checks behind him and slows down smoothly, so as to avoid injury to those on board.

3: He then turns as fast as can be accomplished safely, while looking back down his wake line for the casualty.

4: Steering back into his wake line the helm assesses the wind direction and, once the MOB has been pinpointed, he manoeuvres the yacht to stop upwind of the casualty and across the wind.

5: Using forward and reverse on the engine furthest from the man in the water, he allows the wind to push the yacht sideways towards the MOB.

6: While his remaining crew lasso the casualty, move him back along the leeward side, and then drag him aboard the bathing platform, the skipper stays close to his controls making sure that the engines are in neutral (or switched off) while the MOB is close alongside.

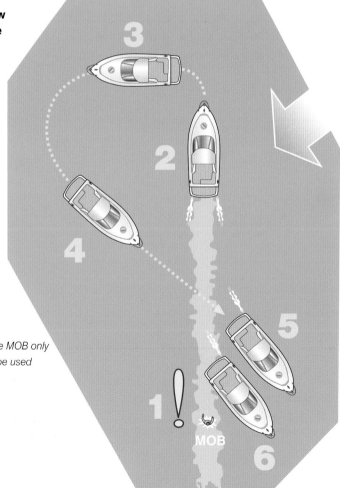

Fig 12:8 When approaching the MOB only the far side engine should be used

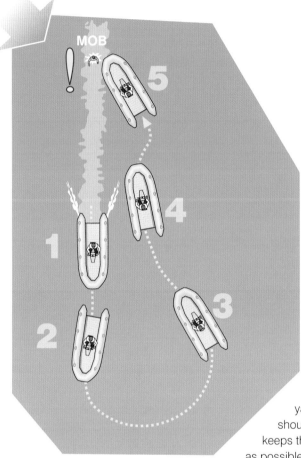

Fig 12:9 Here the MOB is recovered over the bow – as far away as possible from the prop

RIBs and small powerboats

The manoeuvre for RIBs and other small powerboats is very similar to the manoeuvre for large motor yachts except that the final pick up should be on the windward bow. This keeps the MOB as far away from the props as possible and eliminates the risk of a boat with such a shallow draught being blown over him. Another point to consider is the position of the engine controls. If they are on the starboard side of the boat, as in our example, then it's best to roll the casualty back on board on the port side so that the activity on deck is well away from them.

1 & 2: **The helmsman hears the Man Overboard call, slows down gradually and turns back into his wake.**

3 & 4: **Driving back along his wake line, he finds the casualty and then manoeuvres to make a pick up on his port bow with the casualty to windward.**

5: **Once alongside he stops his engines before he and the rest of his crew busy themselves rolling their wet crewmate back on board.**

LIFEBUOYS, DANBUOYS AND LIGHTS

In rough seas throw your danbuoy overboard as soon as possible after the MOB, even if you believe it may be out of his reach. It will give you a point to aim back at if you lose sight of the person and he may be able to swim to it. Any lifebuoy without a danbuoy attached is probably best kept until you are within a reasonable throwing distance of the casualty, most likely as you make your approach. After all, you may have to abort the approach and go around again.

Recovery methods

If your casualty is conscious, stop the boat a few metres away and use a buoyant throwing line to pull him towards the boat. Once alongside, secure the MOB with a loop of rope, so that he can't float away, before lifting. If the casualty is unconscious or simply unable to help, use a loop of rope as a lasso to pull him alongside and secure him.

Once he's alongside, a sailboat with a large crew, or large winches, can simply use a halyard (spinnaker halyards are best) to hoist the casualty on board. Small crews, however, may want to keep a powerful 'block and tackle' handy that can be attached to a spare halyard or a boom to hoist in a heavy casualty. Traditional displacement motor boats with short masts or davits can use similar methods to hoist casualties over their rails while most modern style cruisers have a low

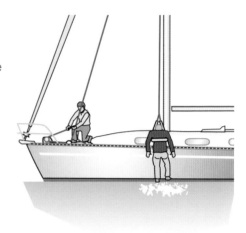

Fig 12:10 A spinnaker halyard can be used to winch the MOB aboard. On some boats you can even use an electric windlass as shown here

bathing platform aft that can be used as a recovery point.

There are a number of proprietary MOB recovery devices on the market, some using buoyant strops, and some working on the parbuckle principle. They all have their pros and cons, but whatever boat type you have, work out a system for hoisting a heavy casualty back aboard that works with your gear and your crew. And then PRACTISE. After all, it may be you.

Fig 12:11 MOB recovery devices come in many forms. A simple buoyant and padded strop is the most common

Treatment of a cold casualty

- Change into dry clothes.
- Re-warm slowly.
- Give warm drinks.
- Use thermal protective aids such as foil blankets to retain body heat.
- Monitor and record reflexes and symptoms.
- Obtain medical assistance if at all in doubt, then have him checked over, once back ashore.

HELICOPTER RESCUE – THE HI LINE TECHNIQUE

- An approaching rescue helicopter will give you a course to steer and a speed based on your boat and the sea state. The message may be passed by radio or by a sign in the aircraft's door. You can anticipate that the course will leave the wind at about 30° off your port bow or as close hauled as possible for a sailing boat. This is because helicopter pilots prefer to hover into the wind and they sit on the starboard side of their cockpits. A sailing boat in rough seas will probably sail under just a jib or genoa. The sails will help dampen any tendency to roll, making it much safer for the winchman.

- Having received your instructions, detail a helmsman to steer a straight steady course and keep looking ahead. Detail another crew to put on gloves and stand by with a bucket.

- The winchman will approach your port side so prepare the landing area by clearing away any gear that can be moved. There will be lots of noise and downdraught.

- The helicopter pilot will dangle a weighted nylon line, first into the water to earth any static electricity and then within your reach. If he doesn't dip the line, grab it anyway (preferably wearing gloves) and flake it into a bucket. DO NOT ATTACH THE LINE TO THE BOAT!

- Use the line to guide the winchman onto the boat. When he arrives he will unhook from the hi-line and take charge.

- When he departs use the light line in gloved hands to control the swing and allow it to pay out freely from the boat.

- Once the helicopter is close, don't use rocket flares or bright lights.

- Use hand held flares when directed by the aircrew.

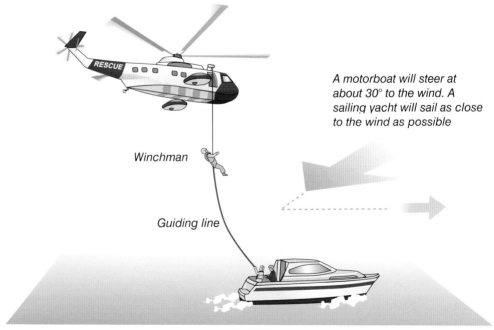

A motorboat will steer at about 30° to the wind. A sailing yacht will sail as close to the wind as possible

Winchman

Guiding line

Fig 12:12

GLOSSARY

ABAFT	Behind, or towards the stern: e.g. abaft the beam
ABEAM	Situated to one side of the boat
AFT	Towards the stern
AHEAD	In front of the boat
AMIDSHIPS (MIDSHIPS)	In the middle of the boat. To put the helm amidships is to centre so the boat steers straight ahead
APPARENT WIND	The wind vector that drives the boat. A combination of the true wind and boat speed
ASTERN	Behind the boat
BACK (to BACK a sail)	Sheeting a sail to windward
BACKSTAY	Standing rigging supporting the mast from the stern
BEAM	The maximum width of the boat
BEAM REACH	Sailing with the wind coming over the beam, at 90° to the wind direction
BEAR AWAY	To turn a boat away from the wind
BERTH	A place to moor, or for someone to sleep
BOLLARD	A strong point to secure a mooring warp, either on the dock or the boat
BOW	The forward part of the boat. Port and Starboard bows are either side of the stem
BOW ROLLER	A fairlead for the anchor warp
BOW THRUSTER	A propeller set in the bow designed to push the bow sideways to port or starboard
BROACH (BROACHING)	An uncontrollable turn into the wind
CATAMARAN	A boat with two separate hulls
CATENARY (of warp)	The curve made by the anchor warp between the stem and the anchor
CLEAT	A 'T' shaped strong point for securing ropes
CLOSE HAULED	Sailing to windward, as close as possible to the wind
CLOSE REACHING.	Sailing a course somewhere between a beam reach and close hauled
COCKPIT	The area sunk below deck level but open to the weather from which a boat is controlled
COLREGS	Colloquial term for the International Regulations for the Prevention of Collision at Sea. IRPCS
DEAD RUN	Sailing directly downwind

DEPOWER	To spill wind from a sail and lose forward speed
DISPLACEMENT	The weight of water displaced by a vessel afloat
DISPLACEMENT MODE	When a vessel is operating without benefit of hydrodynamic lift – i.e. not planing
DOWNTIDE, DOWNSTREAM	To run with the tide or stream
DROGUE	A device designed to create drag – usually streamed astern from a long rope in heavy weather or from a liferaft to help prevent it being blown downwind
DSC	Digital Selective Calling. A system whereby a VHF radio transmitter can make an automatic digitized call to a selected station
FAIRLEAD	A deck fitting used to lead a rope towards a winch or cleat to minimise chafe
FAIRWAY	The main channel into a harbour. That part of an approach channel lying outside of a harbour entrance
FENDERS	Soft (often air-filled) pads hung over a boat's sides to protect it from anything alongside
FENDER BOARDS	Planks with rope ties spanned across a series of fenders to spread their protective effect
FIN KEEL	A deep, narrow, plate type keel, attached to the bottom of a boat on the centreline
FORESTAY	The stay running from the bow to the mast. Primarily to support the mast, but also used to carry genoas and jibs
FREEBOARD	The vertical distance from the waterline to the deck
GAFF	A spar supporting the top edge of a four cornered, fore and aft mainsail
GAFFER	Colloquial name for a boat setting such a sail
GENOA	A foresail that overlaps the mast
HALYARD	A rope used to hoist a sail
HANKED ON	Attaching a sail to a stay with piston or other type of hank
HEAVING TO	Stopping a boat under sail by backing the jib
HEEL	The amount that a boat leans over
HELM	The steering position. The tiller or wheel. The person steering (of either gender)
HELMSMAN	The person steering a vessel
HOVE TO	See HEAVING TO
IRPCS	See COLREGS
ISAF	The International Sailing Associations Federation, the governing body for yacht racing
JIB	Foresail that does not overlap the mast

JIB SHEET	Rope used to control the jib
KICKER, KICKING STRAP	A device – often a simple tackle – intended to prevent the boom from lifting. Sometimes called a VANG
KNOT	One nautical mile per hour
LAZY SHEET	A sheet not in use
LEE SHORE	A shore onto which the wind is blowing
LEECH	The trailing edge of a sail
LEEWARD	The side of the boat facing away from the wind
LEEWARD BERTH	A berth the wind pushes a boat into – i.e. downwind of the boat
LONG KEEL	A keel that runs almost from the bow to the stern of a boat, along the centreline
LUFF	The leading edge of a sail
MAINSAIL	The sail attached to the back of the mast (or main mast if there is more than one)
MAIN SHEET	The rope used to control the angle of the mainsail
MARINA	A collection of berths and other facilities, provided for boaters
MARKED CHANNELS	Navigation channels defined with buoys or beacons
MOB	Man overboard
PILES, PILINGS	Posts driven into the sea bed for securing vessels or as navigational beacons. Also used as protection to stone or concrete walls
PIVOT POINT	The point around which a boat swivels when it is steered
PLANING	Operating a vessel fast, with the hull skidding over the surface of the water rather than through it
POLING	Extending a headsail outboard using a pole
PONTOON	A floating platform used for mooring boats
PORT	The left hand side of the boat looking forward
PORT SIDE TO	Placing the port side of the vessel against a quay or pontoon
PORT TACK	Sailing with wind coming over the port side
POWER UP	Trimming the sail to provide more drive and increase speed
PREVENTER	A line running forward from the boom to the deck used to 'prevent' the boom from swinging across the deck, uncontrolled
QUARTER	The side of a vessel between amidships and the stern
REEFING	Reducing sail area as the wind rises
RIB	A rigid inflatable boat. Usually a small powerboat
RODE	Any arrangement of chain and/or rope used for anchoring
RUNNING BACKSTAYS	A pair of temporary stays used singly to support the mast and provide tension in the forestay, on the windward side of the mainsail
SAR	Search and rescue

SCANDALISE	Spoiling a mainsail's shape, for instance by lifting the boom
SCREW	Colloquial term for propeller
SHEET	A rope that controls a sail
SHEET ON	To pull a sheet in, to trim it
SHROUDS	Rigging supporting the mast from the sides
SKEG	A fixed fin used to support the leading edge of a rudder
SPADE RUDDER	A cantilevered rudder with no skeg or other external support
SPINNAKER POLE	A spar used to support the windward clew of a spinnaker. Also commonly used to sheet the clew of a headsail to windward
SPREADERS	Struts spreading the shrouds away from the mast
STANCHIONS	Vertical posts supporting the guard rails or wires around the deck
STARBOARD	The right hand side of a boat looking forward
STARBOARD TACK	Sailing with the wind coming over the starboard side
STEAMING LIGHT	Forward facing white light visible through an arc of 225°
STEERAGE WAY	The minimum speed required to maintain control of a boat via the rudder
STERN	The rear end of a boat
STREAM	The flow or movement of water, whether caused by current or tide
SURGING (a rope)	Using friction around a cleat, bollard or winch to control a line
TACK	To sail a boat's bow through the wind. Also, the forward bottom corner of a sail
TIDEWAY	Channels where the effects of tidal stream can be felt
TILLER	A steering bar connected to the rudder
TOPPING LIFT	A line running from the end of the boom to the deck via the mast top, used for lifting the boom and supporting it when the mainsail is taken down
TOPSIDES	Sides of the boat between the waterline and the deck
TRANSOM	A flat section of hull across the stern of a boat
TRIM TABS	Adjustable horizontal plates on the stern of a power boat which help control trim
UPTIDE	Upstream, running against the flow of water
VANG	See KICKER
WAKE	The trail of disturbed water left behind a moving boat
WARP	A rope used for mooring or anchoring
WINDAGE	The amount by which a vessel is affected by wind. Also the areas of hull and superstructure that contribute to this effect
WINDWARD (WEATHER)	The side that the wind is coming from
WINDWARD (WEATHER) **BERTH**	A berth that a boat is blown away from

INDEX

A

anchor, 'clubbing'	48
anchor types	76
anchor warp ('rode')	76, 77, 78
anchoring	74-78

see also moorings, stern-to

chain or rope?	76
chart symbols	74
choosing an anchorage	74-75
Colregs	78
coming to anchor	77
raising the anchor	78
rope or chain?	76
sailing to anchor	78
approach, lines of	25-26, 30

see also coming alongside tidal quay;
mooring under sail: approach, best line
of, selecting

between two rafts of yachts	26
astern, going, control principles	14

B

bearings, taking, when mooring	75, 77

see also transits; visual references when
mooring

berthing, lines of approach	25-26

see also coming alongside tidal quay

between two rafts of yachts	26
berthing, slow speed control	18

berthing in marina see marina, entering

boat types see catamarans; motorboats;
RIBs; sailing yachts

boathooks	21
bollards	51
bow thrusters	15,16, 45
bowline	52
broaching	72, 84, 86
buoys, mooring	
making fast	22
picking up	20, 21

see also mooring under sail: approach,
best line of, selecting

securing to	21

Trot mooring see moorings, Trot

C

catamarans	7, 14, 15, 16, 49
chart symbols for anchoring	74
cleats	51
clove hitch	53
Collision Regulations (Colregs)	73, 78, 81
coming alongside tidal quay	23-24

see also berthing, lines of approach;
moorings alongside tidal quay; slow
speed control

control, principles of	13-14
going astern	14
steerable drives and twin screws	14
control, slow speed	18
currents, influence of	8

see also 'ferry glide'; stream, using to
advantage; stream direction indicators

D

danbuoys	98
distress call	92
downwind sailing	71-72
'goose winging'	72
gybing	71
headsails, poling out	72
headsails, twin	72
mainsail use	72
preventers	71
rolling from side to side	71
'dragging' mooring lines	44
drogues	85, 89
Dyneema ropes	50

E

emergencies	90-99
groundings	90-91
checking for damage	91

helicopter rescue 99
lifejackets 92-93
man overboard (MOB)
see man overboard
safety harnesses 92-93
safety hooks 92
engine control, use of neutral 19

F

fast turns 19
'fender, wandering' 39, 57, 58
fender boards 55
fenders, horizontal row 23
'ferry glide' 24, 25, 31, 32, 33, 40, 41, 67
figure of eight knot 52
forces, outside 6

G

'goose winging' 72
groundings 90-91
   checking for damage 91
gybing 71

H

handling characteristics 7
see also motor boats and sailing yachts
entries
headsails, poling out 72
headsails, twin 72
heaving to 70
see also sails, de-powering
helicopter rescue 99
HMPE ropes 50
'hovering' head to stream 15-16, 33

I

International Regulations for the Prevention
of Collision at Sea (Colregs) 73, 78, 81

J

jib, heavy weather 86-87
jib, storm 86, 87, 89

K

'kick, the' see prop walk effect
knots 52-53
   bowline 52

clove hitch 53
figure of eight 52
reef knot 52
rolling hitch 53
round turn and two half hitches 53
sheet bend 52
tugboat hitch 53

L

lassoing buoys 21
leaving a wall or pontoon 27-28
see also marina, leaving
   'springing off' 28
leeway 65, 73
lifebuoys 98
lifejackets 92-93

M

mainsail, 'scandalising' 66
mainsail use downwind 72
man overboard (MOB) 92-98
   danbuoys 98
   distress call 92, 93
   first reactions 92-93
   lifebuoys 98
   Mayday call 92, 93
   motor boats, large 96
   powerboats, small 97
   practising 93, 98
   recovery methods 98
   RIBs 97
   sailing cruisers 94
   sailing yachts with large mainsails,
   running backstays etc. 95
   treatment of cold casualty 98
manoeuvres, basic 15-28
   buoys, making fast 22
   buoys, picking up 20, 21
   see also mooring under sail: approach,
   best line of, selecting
   buoys, securing to 21
   coming alongside tidal quay 23-24
   see also berthing, lines of approach;
   moorings alongside tidal quay; slow
   speed control

'ferry glide' 24, 25, 31, 32, 33, 40, 41, 67
leaving   27-28
see also marina, leaving
'springing off'   28
lines of approach   25-26, 30
   between two rafts of yachts   26
sitting in a tideway   15-16, 33
slow speed control   18
turns, making   16-17
   fast   19
   single screw yachts   16-17
   steerable drives, single   17
   twin screw yachts   17
marina, entering   29-38
  advice, general   38
  downstream   33
  downstream, stop and reverse   34
  finger berths, condition   38
  head to stream   31
   turn first   32
  leeward finger berth, still water   35
  line of approach   30
  mid-ships springs   30, 36, 37
  mooring to floating pontoons   55
  planning   29-30
  VHF channel   30
  visual references   38
  see also transits
  windward finger berth   36
   with stream under pontoon   37-38
marina, leaving   39-46
  downstream exit   41
  gale from ahead   46
  preparations   39
  prop walk effect *see* prop walk effect
  upstream exit   40
  warnings, general   39-41
   downstream exit 41
   upstream exit   40
  warps, using to

advantage   42-43, 44, 45, 46, 48
  see also 'singling up'
  mooring lines; 'springing off'
  wind off the pontoon   45
  wind on the pontoon   43
marina, types of   29
Mayday call   92
momentum, influence of   6, 12, 31, 32, 34
mooring buoys *see* buoys, mooring
mooring lines (warps)   54, 55
  arrival, preparation for   24, 30
  'dragging'   44
  drogue, use as   85, 89
  when leaving   27, 39
  when leaving marina,
  using to advantage   42-43, 44, 45, 46, 48
  mid-ships springs   30, 36, 37, 46, 47, 68
  rafting   62
  'singling up'   27, 39
mooring under sail   63-73
  see also anchoring: sailing to anchor
  approach, best line of, selecting   64-66
  see also approach, lines of
   downwind and upstream   64
   scandalising   66
   upwind and upstream   65-66
  sailing onto quays and pontoons   67-69
   offshore wind just forward
   of the beam   68
   onshore wind ahead   67
   sailing off   69
   'surging'   69
   wind abaft the beam   68
  sails, de-powering   63
moorings   54-62
  alongside tidal quay   54-55
  see also tidal quays, coming alongside
   tidal range   55
  bow-to   60
  floating pontoons   38, 55
  non-tidal   55

rafting   61-62
   leaving a raft   62
   rules   61
   stern-to ('Mediterranean moor') 58-59, 60
      lazy lines   60
   Trot   56-58
      approach for single screw boats   58
      approach for twin engine
      and steerable drive boats   57
motor sailing   73
motorboats
   single screw
      control principles   13
      handling
      characteristics   7,12,13,20,34,43,48
      limitations   48
   steerable drive
      control principles   14
      handling characteristics   7, 14, 38, 49
      limitations   49
      single, making turns   17
   twin screw
      control principles   14
      handling
      characteristics 7, 14, 34, 37, 49
      limitations   49

O

outboards, control with   14, 15, 16
outboards, handling characteristics
and limitations   14, 49

P

'paddle wheel effect'
   see prop walk, influence of
pivot point   8, 13, 36, 47, 48, 49
poling out headsails   72
pontoons, floating, mooring to   38, 55
   see also mooring under sail: sailing
   onto quays and pontoons
preventers   71
prop walk effect
   checking for   12

influence of   6, 11-12, 33, 39, 47
   taming   44
   using to advantage 14, 18, 19, 44, 47, 48
propellers, twin, control principles   14
propellers, use of   13

Q

quays see tidal quays

R

racing yachts, handling characteristics
and limitations   47-48
radio, VHF, DSC facility   92, 93
radio, VHF, marina channel   30
rafting   61-62
   leaving a raft   62
   rules   61
reef knot   52
rescue, helicopter   99
RIBs   38, 49, 97
rolling from side to side   71
rolling hitch   53
ropes   50
round turn and two half hitches   53
rudders, use of   13
   see also steerageway

S

safety harnesses   92-93
safety hooks   92
sailing downwind *see* downwind sailing
sailing yachts
   fin keeled
      handling characteristics 7, 13, 47
      limitations   47
   long keeled
      handling characteristics   7, 48
      limitations   48
   racing, handling characteristics
   and limitations   47-48
   twin keeled
      handling characteristics   7, 47
      limitations   47
sails

de-powering	63
see also heaving to	
head, poling out	72
head, twin	72
heavy weather	86-87, 89
main, scandalising	66
main, use downwind	72
storm	86-87, 89
'scandalising' mainsail	66
sea state	82, 83, 88, 89
sheet bend	52
'singling up' mooring lines	27, 39
slow speed control	18
Spectra ropes	50
'springing off'	28
steerable drives	
control principles	14
handling characteristics	7, 14, 38, 49
limitations	49
single, making turns	17
steerageway	11, 13, 33
storm sails	86, 87, 89
stream, influence of	6, 8
stream, using to advantage	9, 28, 41
see also 'ferry glide'	
stream, wind against: picking up buoys	20, 21
stream direction indicators	8, 20, 24, 39, 64
'surging' the boat	69

T

tidal quays	
coming alongside	23-24
see also berthing, lines of approach; slow speed control	
leaving	27-28
'springing off'	28
mooring alongside 54-55	
see also mooring under sail: sailing onto quays and pontoons	
tidal range	55
tide direction indicators	8, 20, 24, 39
tides, influence of	6, 8
see also stream, using to advantage	
tideway, sitting in	15-16, 33
towing from stern	80, 81
tows, alongside	81
transits	20, 24, 25, 66, 67, 68, 77
see also visual references when mooring	
trysails	86, 87, 89
tugboat hitch	53
turns, making	16-17
fast	19
single screw yachts	16-17
steerable drives, single	17
twin screw yachts	17

V

visual references when mooring	38, 64, 75
see also transits	

W

waves, breaking	84
waves, driving over	88-89
motor yachts	88
sailing yachts	89
weather, heavy	82-89
broaching	72, 84, 86
conditions, variable	83
drogues	85, 89
sails	86-87, 89
waves, breaking 84	
waves, driving over 88-89	
motor yachts 88	
sailing yachts 89	
weather forecasts	83
'wind, apparent'	73
wind, influence of	6, 10-11
wind, steering into or away from	11
wind indicators	10, 39
wind strength	82, 88, 89
windage	10, 45, 49

Promoting and Protecting Boating
www.rya.org.uk

RYA Membership

The RYA is the national organisation which represents the interests of everyone who goes boating for pleasure.

The greater the membership, the louder our voice when it comes to protecting members' interests.

Apply for membership today, and support the RYA, to help the RYA support you.

BENEFITS OF MEMBERSHIP

- Special members' discounts on a range of products and services including boat insurance, books, charts, DVD's and class certificates
- Access to expert advice on all aspects of boating from legal wrangles to training matters
- Free issue of Certificates of Competence, increasingly asked for by everyone from overseas governments to holiday companies, insurance underwriters to boat hirers
- Access to the wide range of RYA publications,including the quarterly magazine
- Third Party insurance for windsurfing members
- Free Internet access with RYA-Online
- Special discounts on AA membership
- Regular offers in RYA Magazine
- ...and much more

JOIN NOW
Membership form opposite or join online at www.rya.org.uk
Visit our website for information, advice, members' services and web shop.

1 **Important** To help us comply with Data Protection legislation, please tick *either* Box A or Box B (you must tick Box A to ensure you receive the full benefits of RYA membership). The RYA will not pass your data to third parties.

A. I wish to join the RYA and receive future information on member services, benefits and offers by post and email.

B. I wish to join the RYA but do not wish to receive future information on member services, benefits and offers by post and email.

When completed, please send this form to: **RYA, RYA House, Ensign Way, Hamble, Southampton, SO31 4YA**

2

Title	Forename	Surname	Date of Birth			Male	Female
			D D	M M	Y Y		
1.							
2.			D D / M M / Y Y				
3.			D D / M M / Y Y				
4.			D D / M M / Y Y				

Address

Town   County   Post Code

Evening Telephone   Daytime Telephone

email

Signature:.................   Date:.................

3 **Type of membership required:** *(Tick Box)*

☐ *Personal*   *Annual rate £39 or £36 by Direct Debit*

☐ *Under 21*   *Annual rate £13 (no reduction for Direct Debit)*

☐ *Family**   *Annual rate £58 or £55 by Direct Debit*

* *Family Membership: 2 adults plus any under 21s all living at the same address*

4 Please tick ONE box to show your main boating interest.

☐ Yacht Racing   ☐ Yacht Cruising
☐ Dinghy Racing   ☐ Dinghy Cruising
☐ Personal Watercraft ☐ Inland Waterways
☐ Powerboat Racing   ☐ Windsurfing
☐ Motor Boating   ☐ Sportsboats and RIBs

Please see Direct Debit form overleaf

RYA

Instructions to your Bank or Building Society to pay by Direct Debit

Please complete this form and return it to:
Royal Yachting Association, RYA House, Ensign Way, Hamble, Southampton, Hampshire SO31 4YA

Originators Identification Number

9	5	5	2	1	3

1. To The Manager: _____ Bank/Building Society

   Address: _____

   _____   Post Code: _____

2. Name(s) of account holder(s)

3. Branch Sort Code

4. Bank or Building Society account number

5. RYA Membership Number (For office use only)

6. **Instruction to pay your Bank or Building Society**
   Please pay Royal Yachting Association Direct Debits from the account detailed in this instruction subject to the safeguards assured by The Direct Debit Guarantee.
   I understand that this instruction may remain with the Royal Yachting Association and, if so, details will be passed electronically to my Bank/Building Society.

   Signature(s) _____

   Date _____

Banks and Building Societies may not accept Direct Debit instructions for some types of account

Cash, Cheque, Postal Order enclosed   £ _____
Made payable to the Royal Yachting Association

077	**Office use only:** Membership Number Allocated

Office use / Centre Stamp

Welcome to The Green Blue

Whether you are a sailor, motor boater or manage a boat-related business, The Green Blue has a raft of helpful environmental information for you.

Top Tips

Oil and Fuel Spills - Use spill kits to clean up oil and fuel spills and keep an oil absorbent in your bilge.

Antifouling and marine paints - Keep unnecessary anti-fouling out of the water when renewing. Don't leave a cvoloured patch under your boat!

Waste Management - Dispose of rubbish responsibly and in the correct container (general or hazardous). Recycle where possible.

Cleaning and Maintanance - Use environmentally friendly cleaning products.

Resource efficiency - Consider how you will dispose of a product before you buy it.

Effects on Wildlife - Find out if anchorages you visit are designated and what this means.

A good starting point is our website: www.thegreenblue.org.uk. It is full of information on how you can limit your impact on the environment.

Register on line to receive a free waterproof copy of the **'Green Blue Guide'** to environmentally sound boating and watersports.

If you are involved in a club or boat-related business, you can read our **Environmental Code of Practice** which gives useful pointers on areas like how to deal with boating waste by visiting **www.ecop.org.uk**

Most people appreciate that we can no longer take our beautiful coastlines for granted. Each time we clean our boat, start our engine or pump out our bilges, we may be allowing chemicals to enter the water. The good news is that by taking a few simple precautions, your conscience can be as clean as your boat!

Brought to you by:

Supported by:

The Green Blue
RYA House
Ensign Way
Hamble
Hants SO31 4YA

Tel: 023 8060 4100